✦ ✦ ✦ ✦   THE SONG OF ÆRTHUR

THE SONG OF ARTHUR

Celtic Tales from the High King's Court

John Matthews

with illustrations by
STUART LITTLEJOHN

A publication supported by
THE KERN FOUNDATION

Quest Books
Theosophical Publishing House
Wheaton, Illinois ◆ Chennai (Madras), India

The Theosophical Society acknowledges with gratitude the generous support of the Kern Foundation for the publication of this book.

First Quest Edition 2002

The Theosophical Publishing House
P. O. Box 270
Wheaton, IL 60189-0270

Cover and text design and typesetting by Beth Hansen-Winter

Library of Congress Cataloging-in-Publication Data

Matthews, John.

The song of Arthur: Celtic tales from the high king's court / John Matthews; with illustrations by Stuart Littlejohn. — 1st Quest ed.
    p.   cm.

ISBN 0-8356-0809-3

1. Arthurian romances—Adaptations.   2. Bards and bardism—Fiction.
3. Mythology, Welsh—Fiction.   4. Taliesin—Adaptations.   I. Title.

PR6063.A86325 S65 2002
823'.914—dc21

2002069993

5   4   3   2   1   *   02   03   04   05   06   07

Printed in the United States of America

To Ardan
  for the gift of Awen

CONTENTS

ACKNOWLEDGMENTS

arious people have helped and encouraged me during the long gestation of this book. They include Geoffrey Ashe, Rosemary Sutcliffe, David Jones, Janet Piedelato, Peter Lamborne Wilson, John Boorman, David Spangler, Kathleen Raine, Ari Berk, and R. J. (Bob) Stewart. To all of these, named and unnamed, I give my thanks and offer the hope that you might like something at least of what is included here. ❧ I should also like to thank Stuart Booth, of the sadly defunct Blandford Press and later Cassell, who saw several of these stories into print and encouraged me to write more. A special thank you, reflected in the dedication of this book, goes to Steve Gladwin, whose adaptation of *The Song of Taliesin* for a remarkable one-man stage show prompted me to return to these earlier writings and to make revisions sufficient to bring them up to the mark. Gratitude also goes to Larry Mendlesburg, whose request for a list of my Arthurian stories for his indispensable bibliography on the subject was largely instrumental in prompting me to put this collection together. Finally, thanks to my editor and friend Brenda Rosen, whose instant love for the stories brought them to the attention of Quest Books. Once there, Sharron

Brown Dorr, a wonderful storyteller herself, helped them into print. As he did for *The Song of Taliesin*, Stuart Littlejohn has produced some memorable drawings for this book. My thanks to him for his patience and care.

INTRODUCTION:
THE KING AND THE BARD

Two figures are central to the stories you are about to read. They are the great British hero Arthur and the Welsh bard Taliesin, who became part of his legend. The former we know best today as "King" Arthur, the mighty and magical monarch whose epic adventures, together with those of his Fellowship of the Round Table, are the subject of a vast array of books, movies, poems, music, and plays which continue to be enjoyed and studied to this day. ❧ But the phenomenon of Arthurian literature and tradition is not a new one. In 1174, the medieval writer Alanus de Insulis, wrote:

> *Whither has not flying fame spread and familiarized the name of Arthur the Briton, even as far as the empire of Christendom extends? Who, I say, does not speak of Arthur the Briton, since he is almost better known to the peoples of Asia than to the Britanni [Welsh and Irish], as our palmers returning from the East inform us? The Eastern peoples know of him, as do the Western, though separated by the width of the whole earth . . . Rome, queen of cities, sings his deeds, nor are Arthur's wars unknown to her former rival Carthage. Antioch, Armenia, Palestine celebrate his acts.* (Prophetia Anglicana Merlini Amrosii Britanni)

Despite being known to the entire civilized world, then as now, Arthur himself remains an elusive figure. Primarily he is a Celtic hero, and it is as a Celt and as part of the Celtic world that he is largely presented in this collection. The historical origins of the king and his warriors are themselves shrouded in myth. The legends tell that he was the son of King Uther Pendragon and the Lady Igraine of Cornwall and that his birth was made possible through the magical arts of the magician Merlin, or *Myrddin* as he is called in the stories that follow, who later became his advisor in all things. History, however, allows him no such romantic heritage; it grants him no known parents, no wizard counselor, no band of shining knights. But what it does suggest is, in its own way, just as remarkable.

Arthur was born, so far as we can tell, sometime in the fifth or sixth century, either in Wales, the Midlands, or Cornwall, and he became, not a great king, but an equally great war leader with the title *Dux Brittanorum*, Duke of Britain. As such, he commanded the armies of the various petty kings and chieftains who had reasserted their claims to the land after the last vestiges of Roman rule came to an end in the previous century. Endlessly quarrelling, continuously raiding each other's lands for the sheer sport of it, these local rulers would have fallen easy victim to incoming Saxon invaders had it not been for Arthur, who persuaded the warring factions to unite against a common foe and to place him at the head of an army drawn from every part of the land.

Precisely how he succeeded in his military campaign against the Saxons is not recorded, nor are many of his subsequent deeds. He seems to have led a band of mounted cavalry, perhaps the original "Knights of the Round Table," whose mobility enabled them to strike deep into the territory held by the enemy, withdraw as swiftly as they had come, and appear again many miles distant to strike at another foe. Such use of cavalry, learned, perhaps, from Roman military methods, must have given Arthur and his men an almost magical status among his own forces as well as among his foes. It must have been these deeds that caused the legendary tales to begin to take shape.

A series of great battles was recorded, their sites now difficult to identify. In these accounts, we learn that Arthur, bearing a shield with the image of the Virgin Mary painted upon it, led his warriors against the Saxons to such good effect that what began as a Saxon invasion ended as a more or less peaceful settlement. The invaders were penned within certain areas of the country, where they were able to farm the land and, in time, intermarry with local folk, thus founding the people known as the "English," a mixture of Celt and Saxon, which remained unchanged until the coming of the Normans in the eleventh century.

The battles led by Arthur had a profound effect on the subsequent history of Britain and, indeed, on the story of Arthur himself. Many Britons fleeing the Saxon invaders found sanctuary across the sea in Brittany, a peninsula of north-west France, thus opening up a channel of communication for the transmission of oral tales from Britain to continental Europe. These stories, we must believe, included many whose hero was Arthur. Some five hundred years later, these same tales returned to Britain in the form of stories and songs told by Anglo-Norman *conteurs*. They became the foundation for the medieval romances on which most of the later Arthurian tradition is based.

Thus the wandering British bards and storytellers who fled the war-torn land did more than anyone to keep the Arthurian legends green and growing. Of the few whose names have survived, one towers above all the rest—Taliesin. It is in his voice that many of the stories that follow are told—as though we, as privileged listeners, are able to sit in one of the great smoke-filled halls of Dark Age Britain and hear silence fall as the bard rises to speak, striking chords on his harp for dramatic emphasis, sometimes breaking into song as he recounts the deeds of Arthur and his warriors.

We know little of Taliesin historically, except that he probably lived in the sixth century and was thus a contemporary of Arthur. Some seventy poems attributed to him have survived, together with a fantastic story (retold in the companion book to this one, *The Song of Taliesin*) of his initiation into a select group of adepts known as "the Cauldron Born," who had imbibed wisdom and inspiration from a drink brewed in the magical cauldron of the goddess Ceridwen, patroness of bards. As with Arthur, stories of the great bard, who was known as the Primary Chief Bard of the Island of Britain, grew and were added to. Inevitably, the time came when Taliesin began to be associated with Arthur. It seemed only right that the greatest of the bards should serve the greatest of kings, and since references to Arthur were to be found in poems attributed to Taliesin, the connection seemed implicit.

The final link in this chain of interconnected traditions came with the association of Taliesin and Merlin, particularly in the medieval *Life of Merlin* by Geoffrey of Monmouth. One of the central figures in the Arthurian epic, Merlin was known in Wales as *Myrddin* and known also to have been a bard. Several of his poems have survived and are similar in style to those of Taliesin. The two were described as engaging in a dialogue, in poetic form, vying with each other in declaring inspired prophetic utterances. Later still, Taliesin was recognized as, in some sense, the successor to Merlin, and he is presented as such in *The Song of Taliesin* and in the stories collected here.

With the coming of the Normans in 1066, the Arthurian epic changed direction. No longer the preserve of the wandering bards, the stories became a literary theme, with dozens of romances, written at first in verse, later on in prose, recounting new adventures and adding new characters and heroes to the ancient Celtic war band. The first writer consciously to draw on the still largely oral sources pertaining to Arthur was a twelfth-century cleric named Geoffrey of Monmouth, who had already collected a book of prophecies attributed to Merlin. He created a vehicle for the seemingly inexhaustible supply of stories concerning the exploits of Arthur and his heroes by writing a *History of the Kings of Britain* which, though it deals also with such semi-historical figures as King Lear, Cassivellaunus, and Constantine, allocates more than half its total pages to the lives of Arthur and Merlin.

Geoffrey's book became a bestseller of its time, with countless manuscript copies made and distributed throughout England and the rest of Europe. Although his veracity as a historian was attacked, even by his near contemporaries, who referred to him as a "fabulator" and a "writer of lies," there is more than a kernel of truth in what Geoffrey wrote. As a source for many of his stories, he claimed to have partially "translated" an ancient book in the British tongue, although no trace of the original has ever been discovered. Whatever the truth of the matter, there can be no doubt that Geoffrey pulled together strands of oral tradition, historical memory, and pure invention, and dressed them in the fashions and settings of his time. In doing so he created the first "Arthurian novel" and set his seal upon the literary career of his hero for several ages to follow.

But behind the literary figure of Arthur who followed from Geoffrey's medieval version of the legend, the more ancient figure of the Celtic Arthur lived on, enshrined in the very landscape. Later writers recorded the still potent presence of Arthur in the places named after him: Arthur's Seat, Arthur's Stone, Arthur's Oven. During the Middle Ages, a gravestone in Wales marked the resting place of his son, Amr; if the stone was moved during one day, the next, it was found back in its original place the following day. Also in Wales, a rocky outcrop is said to bear the print of Arthur's hound, Cabal. In 1184, Arthur's own grave, referred to in an ancient Welsh poetic fragment as "an unwise thought" that should not even be contemplated, was supposedly discovered at Glastonbury, a place long identified with the mystical realm of Avalon.

The unlikely discovery of an actual grave conflicts with the myth of the king who will return. On this hope much of Arthur's enduring fame relies. In twelfth-century Brittany, the same Alanus de Insulis quoted above wrote that anyone venturesome enough to suggest that Arthur might be dead would be stoned by the people, who loved their heroic liberator and believed in his return. This myth of the return of the king has in no way died out, for Arthur continues to live in the hearts of people everywhere.

Thus the real Arthur retains the qualities of the mythic archetype, and it seems appropriate that much of the action of these stories takes place in a mystical realm, specifically in the confines of the great forest of Broceliande, referred to throughout as "the Wood." Broceliande is both an actual place, located physically in present-day Brittany, and a metaphysical reality that represents the world and the place of humanity within it. The heroes and heroines of the Arthurian legends wander in this vast enclave, here perceived as covering most of Britain, where adventures await and creatures fair and foul lurk to threaten those who dare to venture off the beaten track. This place, where all dreams begin, is seen as the heart of Arthur's kingdom, which is here called by its ancient name of *Logres*. The name comes from early Welsh texts, which call Britain *Lloegyr*, after the mythological king Locrinus. This name later became Latinized as *Loegria* and afterwards by Norman French authors as *Logres*.

As in *The Song of Taliesin*, I have adopted the device of a fictional "collector" of the stories. In the previous book, it was a nameless monk who knew Taliesin and recorded his words. Here, the collector is another monk by the name of Joscelyn, who is seen as living around the middle of the thirteenth century, rather than in sixth-century Britain as did Taliesin's scribe. As the first story in the book reveals, it is Joscelyn who "discovers" the manuscripts of the stories and gathers them into a volume. As before, this device has enabled me to provide comments that explain obscure references without interrupting the narrative flow. Joscelyn's comments also suggest something of the changing attitude of the medieval clerics who did, indeed, gather together much of the oldest Arthurian literature.

As with the previous collection, I have placed a selection of original "bardic" poems and songs between each of the tales as a kind of antithesis to the prose texts. Most of these interludes follow the themes of the stories.

Some, but not all, of these stories have appeared in print before. They represent the fruits of a thirty-year obsession with the Arthurian legends, an obsession which, I am glad to say, shows no sign of abating. These stories are, in fact, glimpses into a much larger universe, a universe which I have been exploring, now, for much of my life.

Almost all these stories are based, in one way or another, on texts dating from the eighth to the fifteenth centuries, which together make up the sources for most of what we know of Arthur today. For those who like to know such things,

I have included notes at the back of the book to draw attention to the original sources and to later, literary retellings and to explain references in the stories to earlier myths and mysteries. In every case, however, I have made free with the originals and adapted or altered them as I thought fit.

In part, this collection is a glimpse into a world still in creation. Those who have read *The Song of Taliesin* (revised edition, Quest Books, 2001; originally published, Thorsons, 1991) may find points of connection between the two; the very assiduous will see where there are even more divergences. One day, if spared, I shall complete my vast Arthurian work, *Broceliande*, and then the connections between all of these tales will be clearer. For now, I hope that the many Arthurian fans and friends who have asked me repeatedly when I would be finished may be partly mollified by this collection. At least I did not let the new millennium get too old without putting something together!

John and Caitlín Matthews offer workshops in Celtic Shamanism and Arthurian Mysteries all over the world. For information, upcoming publications, and news, see their website Hallowquest.org.uk.

Part I
EARLY TALES

1

JOSCELYN'S TALE

he only pleasure we are supposed to have is the love of God. It should be enough to serve him, to follow his way. But I must confess that I have known another pleasure in my years at the abbey of Ynys Witrin— the pleasure given by books. ❧ Not just the Great Book by which we all live our lives between these walls, but books that many consider at best, foolish, and at worst, dangerous. I mean by this, books of stories. Not, of course, that the Great Book does not itself contain many stories of wonder and beauty: Who is not moved by the tale of Daniel in the lion's den or of Moses walking upon the floor of the sea? But the stories I refer to are of another kind. I mean stories of heroes, of adventure, of human love. Even of magic—though many will cower and cross themselves at the very mention of this word. ❧ Many, I know, consider it sinful to mention such things. But I have learned a surprising fact: that one may learn a great deal from such stories, and that not all of what one learns is wicked and sinful, as many would have us believe. I have learned that not all who failed to live their lives by the Great Book are necessarily evil. After all, it was

an accident of birth that brought them into the world in the days before Our Lord walked the earth. Nor should we forget that it is said that "He went down into the deep places of the earth to free those who had gone before."

Abbot Thomas, who when I first came to this house, ruled over us with a firm but kindly hand, told me that I am wrong to think these things, but he himself had a tale to tell that bears out my belief. I shall speak of his tale hereafter. But mostly I write these words because I, too, have a story to tell—one that I know in my heart that I must relate, even if it incurs the wrath of my superiors and places my immortal soul in danger. It is part of a greater story, which must also be told.

If Brother Timothy had not told me, on a day more than thirty years ago now, to gather the old, dusty vellum and parchments stored in a dark corner of the scriptorium and to scrape them clean for reuse, I might never have found the stories of the bard Taliesin and the hero-king Arthur.

The abbey was a storehouse of books and scrolls, gathered by assiduous abbots determined to make the library of Ynys Witrin the finest in Britain. The discards from these acquisitions, deemed of little value, ended up in the scriptorium. There, among the dust and spider webs, lay the accumulation of decades of such collecting, piled high and haphazardly. And there, amongst the rest, I found a bundle wrapped in oiled cloth.

At first I was prompted simply to discard it, but having been blessed—or cursed—with an insatiable curiosity, I unrolled the bundle and found myself holding a thick, untidy bundle of papers of all shapes and sizes; some of them roughly made, others refined. Many were stained, and in some, the writing which covered them densely was faded or illegible. One sentence, however, stood out from the rest. My eye was drawn to it, and I read: "I have learned to love God only slowly and with difficulty." Something about these words touched a place in my own heart, for I, too, have not always found the path an easy one.

The writing was crabbed and difficult, and it was in a dialect of the Old People of this land which few now speak. Perhaps it was fate that I am one who does so, for I was born on the borders of England and Wales, where many remember the

BROTHER JOSCELYN

history of Y Gogledd, and where the Old Tongue is spoken by children from birth. Of course, in the monastery, I had learned Latin, and this I speak mostly now, but as I looked at the words written in the language of my fathers, I felt tears spring to my eyes as the familiar sounds played again in my mind. Though the language was at times oddly phrased, I found I could decipher it easily enough.

I read on: "I am setting down the things I have gathered here, making, as it were, a heap of all I can find. The story of how I met the Lord Taliesin is a part of it, and is best told here, at the beginning."

It was the name that caught my attention. *Taliesin.* I had seen it before, in one of the countless manuscripts over which I had poured under the tutelage of Brother Anselm, my old novice master, who had seen something in me that he thought might one day turn into a scholar's gift. For a moment I searched my memory, then shrugged and read on.

What I found was a story that both fascinated and excited me. I read how the scribe, whose name never appears in the collection of his writings, met with the great bard, who was perhaps the last of his kind, and at his bidding began to collect and write down an entire lifetime of stories—some of which, at least, I now held in my hands. Lost to all sense of time and filled with a rising excitement, I leafed through the untidy bundle of papers, while a sentence here, a name or word there, leapt out at me. One name in particular, appeared frequently—Arthur.

This name I knew well, indeed, as did all of us who were part of the community of Ynys Witrin. Here, more than eighty years ago now, a brother digging a fresh grave had discovered a huge coffin, on which there was a lead cross inscribed with the words: *HIC JACET ARTURUS IN INSULA AVALONIS*, or in the common speech, "Here Lies Arthur in the Island of Avalon." This find had caused a stir of excitement such as is seldom seen in the cloisters of this or any abbey. If this were truly the grave of the greatest hero ever to live in the land of Britain, it was news indeed. Further investigation revealed a skeleton of prodigious size, and a smaller one, evidently that of a woman, laid beside it. The monk who opened it later declared that a hank of fine golden hair had fallen to dust when he tried to pick it up. (Later it was said that these bones belonged to Arthur's queen, Gwenhwyfar, but I myself doubt this.)

In my own time, some five years past, King Edward himself visited the abbey and, since he claimed descent from Arthur himself, ordered the bones to be reinterred in a great black marble tomb which stands now before the high altar of our church. Many pilgrims come here to stare with curiosity at the last resting place of the great king.

As I read on through the manuscript, all thought of my original task forgotten, I saw many references to Arthur and slowly it dawned upon me that I had stumbled on something of great importance. I also felt close to the nameless scribe, who described himself as a monk, and who had apparently written the words I was reading. It seemed as though his mind reached out across the years to touch mine, whispering an urgent plea that his words be heard by others.

With trembling hands I restored the original wrapping to the bundle of papers and hurried in search of Abbot Thomas. I found him in his cell, and as so often, on his knees, and waited with rising impatience while he completed his devotions. As soon as he rose to his feet, I thrust the bundle of parchments at him, words spilling from my mouth as I sought to tell him of my discovery.

After a moment Abbot Thomas held up his hands.

"Peace, my son. Begin at the beginning."

I did so, and as I told my story and spread the parchments before him, I saw a light in his eyes that I had never seen there before. It was a look of wonder and delight, and it changed his usually grave face so that for a moment I saw the boy that still lived somewhere within him. When I fell silent at last, he began to examine the writings, turning over the pages gently and studying them with great attention. Born in the same part of the country as myself, he was able to read them. Finally, he looked up at me.

"My son, you have made a discovery of great importance, both to the abbey and to this land." He paused, looking down at tumbled pages for a moment. Then he said: "Say nothing of this to anyone."

His words astonished me. If, as I rightly believed, and as he himself suggested, the documents lying before us were as important as they seemed, why hide their existence?

Seeing my bewilderment, Abbot Thomas did his best to reassure me.

"I cannot explain my reason for this request at the moment, my son, but I ask you to follow my wishes—not because of your vow of obedience, but because I ask it in good faith. In addition, I have a task for you—one which I believe you will not find difficult. These papers must be put in order and a copy made. I want you to undertake this, and I want you to do so in secret." His next words echo still in my thoughts as I write. "I ask you to do this so that the voice of tradition may be heard again."

It was to be years before I understood these words. To a great extent, they are my reason for writing this account of my discovery—that and a sense of comradeship with my brother in Christ who first set down the words of the Lord Taliesin.

So began a time of great strangeness—and of great wonder. It is no easy thing for a brother to hide anything from the rest of the community, and often I found myself longing to share my secret with another. But the abbot's words were ever in my mind, and I held them to be a sacred trust—as, indeed, I did the papers I had found.

Many of the pages I had found, despite their careful wrapping, had grown brittle with age and the ink so faded that there were times when I was hard pressed to read them. Abbot Thomas' request that they be copied out again was clearly a good one, but first I had to find enough material to write upon, for vellum was scarce and valuable, and every scrap had to be accounted for. Fortunately—or perhaps because Abbot Thomas requested it—Brother Timothy gave me the task of completely reordering the moldering heaps of paper and skins among which I had made my discovery. Every day for several months, I made my way into the dark and musty area behind the scriptorium and began the task of sorting the ancient parchments into piles—those for reuse, those for discarding. Secretly, however, I made a third heap, gathering the best and most usable vellum together so that I might make my own use of it to copy the manuscript I had found.

Words do not come easily to me, and I am in awe not only of the great bard himself but also of my ancient brother, who seemed able to fit words together more subtly than I shall ever do. As nearly as I can explain it, I found that the tales fell into two groups: those which were most clearly the work of the little monk, and those which—though, perhaps, deriving from a different source— nonetheless had to do with the adventures of the great King Arthur.

The first group were, it seemed, written by the little monk from the dictation of his Master; while others may even have been written out by the great bard himself, since most speak directly to the ear and contain none of the asides to "the little monk" that are scattered through the rest. These I gathered into what I hope will one day become a single volume.

Still others I found, gathered together with the rest, that seem to have been added later. These, I have convinced myself, whether truly or not, might have been favorite tales of the bard, maybe even those that he told in the circle of the great court of Camelot. But they are written in several others' hands and, I now believe, at different times. Perhaps their source is amongst the keepers of these writings; one or another has added tales he felt belonged there, even though they might not have been written by Taliesin himself or copied by the little monk. Some of these I have grouped under the heading "Fugitive Tales" in this collection, since I am uncertain as to their origin, or even of their connection to the history of the Lord Arthur. Maybe others who read these in some other time will understand their place better than I and make of them more than I ever could.

When I had sufficient material to begin my task, I found ways to escape from the round of work which delineated our lives in the abbey. Often I sat up deep into the night, working by a scrap of candle hidden beneath my robe, missing the few hours of sleep between *nones* and *tierce*. Looking back on this time, it is a wonder to me that I was not discovered, or that I did not become ill from lack of sleep. Certainly my eyes grew almost permanently red-rimmed from pouring over the crabbed writing of the little monk and the even older and more difficult writing of the great bard.

Of course, I had also to find a hiding place for both the original writings and my own copies. After searching for such a place for several weeks (during which time I concealed the bundle of manuscripts beneath my mattress, in constant fear of its being discovered) I finally hit upon a plan. One of the stones in the inner wall of my cell was loose, and with a little effort, I was able to prize it out. Behind, as I had hoped, was a small space, and there I hid the oiled bundle—soon joined by a growing number of sheets covered by my own script.

In the end, some eight months later, my labors were finished. Many times I was almost discovered, and I thought that brothers Timothy and Anselm often looked at me askance, as though they knew that I was somehow disobeying the rule of our Order, though they could not prove it. Now, I believe I was in some way protected, that God wanted my to finish the work and to keep the secret—or maybe that Abbot Thomas' prayers were strong enough to protect me.

But, in the end, the task was complete, and I sought out Abbot Thomas to show him what I had accomplished. As before, I saw delight transform his face as he poured over my work. I notice that he never lingered long enough to read more than a word here and there, enough to see that I had written clearly. I wondered at this, since one of the greatest joys my labor had given me was to share the stories, strange and wonderful and often heretical though they seemed.

When he had finished, the abbot sat in silence for a while, eyes closed as though in prayer. Then, at last, he looked up at me.

"Brother Joscelyn, this is a wondrous gift that you have given the abbey—and, if God wills it, many others in time." He paused, then continued slowly:

"You have done well to master your curiosity. I promise that there will come a day when all shall be made clear to you. For the moment . . . ." He rose and crossed to the carved oak chest that stood against one wall. Opening it he took out a number of folded pages of parchment. Handing these to me, he said: "This is part of the story also. Perhaps when you read it, you will feel that it belongs with the writings you have so faithfully gathered. Ponder it carefully, and maybe you will understand something of my part in this great enterprise."

Filled with curiosity, I asked what was to become of the writings.

"Keep them safe as you have kept them through these months," Abbot Thomas replied. "Tell no one of these things until the time is right. You will know when that is."

He gave me a blessing then, and I hurried back to my cell to read the pages he had given me. There I read the story which is here called "Thomas and the Book." As I did so, it came to me that this was his own story, though I could not be certain, then or now, and that within it lay a clue to the mystery of my own discovery. But even then I did not fully understand. It was to be many years later, when Abbot Thomas lay on his deathbed, that I finally knew the truth. My own hair was grayer by then, and long hours in the cold and draughty church had caused my joints to grow stiff. Yet, in all that time, I had kept my word and spoken to no one of my discovery.

Hours before his death, Abbott Thomas called me to his bedside, banishing all others from the room while he spoke to me alone. I saw more than one curious, even jealous, look on the faces of my brethren, but they obeyed the dying man's request and left us alone.

Abbott Thomas beckoned me close. His voice was a mere thread, but there was an urgency in him that I knew must be consuming his failing strength.

"My son, it is time you knew the truth, for so it has been passed on from one to another since the passing of the king."

I felt the hair on the back of my neck rise up at these words. Abbot Thomas reached out and caught my hand in a surprisingly strong grip.

"In the days after King Arthur went away, the land lay in great trouble. Many there were who wished to blot out his name forever. But the bard whose words you read and studied when you first discovered the writings of the little monk made a great book, written in the British tongue, in which he set down all that had passed in those strange, far-off days. This work he entrusted to the monk who had become his scribe before he, too, vanished from the eyes of men. When the little monk himself died, that book, along with the papers which you discovered, were hidden. How they came to this place I do not know. Perhaps there were already stories which told of the burial of the great king here—though others tell that he is not dead at all, but sleeping in the Otherworld."

The old man paused, and we both instinctively made the sign of the cross. Then Abbot Thomas continued.

"When I first came to Ynys Witrin, the abbot of that time was already old. I know not what he saw in me, but when his time came, he named me his successor, and before he died told me the secret of this place. The ancient book was here—hidden safely where no one would ever find it save by being shown where it was. The dying abbot told me that it was to remain in hiding until a distant time when the land was settled. Alas, this has not yet come to pass. The papers you discovered must once have been kept together with the bard's greater work. Somehow they became separated, maybe hidden and then forgotten, until you, my son, found them and restored them to us. Now, I pass this sacred trust to you, that the voice of tradition may be heard when the time is right."

Having read the story of that other Thomas (if, indeed, he was other than the man who lay before me) I recognized these words as a reference to the mysterious

Voice which had spoken to him. But now, drawing upon the last of his strength, the dying abbot spoke again, his voice never rising above a whisper, and revealed to me the hiding place of the bard's ancient book. That secret I have kept until this day and will keep it still until I seek out the one who will be my successor. I have read the last great work of the Lord Taliesin, and it has changed me forever, as I believe it must change anyone who reads it. But I wish also to pay homage to the little monk, who speaks to me sometimes still, across the years, whispering in my ear that his words should be better known.

And so, I have taken the decision to gather up these pages that I copied, long years ago, and to send them to another, whom I have entrusted with this task, and who will arrange for them to be properly bound into two volumes. Afterwards I shall see to it that these are placed on the shelves of the library, for during my time I have done my own share of work to fulfill the dreams of other abbots—to make Ynys Witrin a center for learning.

I do not know who will read these pages, nor when. Yet I believe that, though there are many strange and terrible things described in them, yet the light of God shines through them, and that one day they will be seen by others and read with understanding of the great and wonderful deeds that took place in that magical age.

As for the ancient book, that must remain where it is hidden until it is revealed to one who keeps it that the time has indeed come to bring it into the light. That will not happen in my time, for my own death is not far off. Still, I am glad to know that my love of books, so frowned upon by others in my order, gave me the opportunity to serve the voice of tradition. It certainly gave me great joy, for the words of the great bard are within my thoughts, and daily I recall them along with the prayers and words of our own Great Book. I no longer feel guilty at this, for I have learned that the old tales are filled with a power that is too important to be forgotten, and I believe that it will live on, perhaps even until time itself is rolled up, and we are all received into the peace of our Lord God and his Son.

SONG OF THE GRAIL LORD

I sing of the stranger who is Lord of the Grail.
Pushing against the clouded walls of the world,
The night trembles and shakes as he moves,

Dark centers shift and merge in the darkness of the Wood.
Between the twisted shapes of memory, twilight
Rises like a cloud of dust—the morning falls choked and dead.
Power holds me caught in a net of spider webs
Drawing me towards the lip of the abyss.
I cry, but my cry goes unheard on the dizzy edge.

A moist wind drags at the mind's limit,
And the form I wear begins to melt,
Trickling like smoke in the gray air.

Irresistibly drawn I move towards the dark
Knowing as I do that the dark itself
Draws nearer to a darker night.

I forget, and forget again as the shapes change,
Forget that I am drawn in a moving urge,
A desire to return to the flame of creation.

I sing of the Lord who is master of the Grail,
Trusting that I move
Outward from the darkness of my world,

To learn again the secrets of Caer Siddi.

2

THE KINGLY SHADOW

There have always been kings in these lands. Sometimes seen and sometimes unseen. But always, it seems to me, there is the right man waiting to come forward at the right time. If one failed to do so, a surrogate would be found. Often he ruled as well as any man and was none the worse for not being the true king. But still, only when the true and rightful heir steps upon the King Stone is the land truly preserved. That is the way it has always been and that is the way it will always be. ❧ In the time of which I speak, some knew, by signs and portents in the heavens, that a king more great than any seen so far was soon to come. The druids had seen it long since, and the college of priests, who studied the heavens daily from their great foundation in the City of the Legions, had begun to suspect that it might be so. One especially, whose name was Myrddin, had been appointed by the dwellers in Avalon to seek out the new king and see to it that he found his throne and his true destiny. For he that was coming was to be King Before and King Hereafter; he had ruled before and died, and now was about to be reborn. This time, it was said, he would not die, but return instead to

Avalon when the moment came, there to await a time when he would be needed by the land.

These are very great mysteries of which the great bard speaks. I have heard it said that in the time before the coming of Christ to these islands, the king to be would enter into congress with a woman who embodied the power of the earth within herself. This strange marriage between the king and the land betokened the contract between the monarch and the patch of earth over which he ruled. It was considered the deepest betrayal for any man to fail to honor this unwritten charter. In some of the tales that I have read, it is implied that the Ymerawdwr, or "emperor," as many at the time called the great King Arthur, was at fault in this way for not honoring his bride Gwenhwyfar, and that this failing brought about the downfall of the kingdom he established. But of this I may not speak with any true authority. It seems to me also that a tale I found among the oldest of the scrolls, which I have here called "The Third Awakening," tells more of these things. The thought of a man born again and again to serve as king causes me to shiver whenever I think of it. I shall pray for his soul daily and hope that he may find rest at last in the Heavenly Realm.

The man who ruled over most of Britain at this time was named Ambrosius Aurelianus, in the Roman fashion. He wore the toga with the wide, purple stripe that signified nobility, had his chin and checks shaved for him, and wore his hair short. But for all that, it was known that his mother was of the Silures, so that he had the royal blood of the Maiden in his veins, as well as the iron blood of Rome. Thus he was at least halfway fit to rule, even though he was not the chosen king and had not married the land.

Those were troubled times, as you may recall, when the legions had been called away to save the floundering empire, and when the chieftain Gwytheryn, he of the thin lips, had invited the Saxon hounds into our land, at first to fight against the Picti and the Scotti, but soon enough they began to help themselves to lands and to plunder wherever they wished, so that they were no longer merce-naries, but invaders.

At first there was little resistance, for in that time there was more interest among the warrior kindred to fight each other than to defend the whole of the land. So that when the people saw how Ambrosius began to organize forces and unite the feuding tribes against their common enemy, and how he seemed to represent the best of Rome and of Britain, they were not slow to follow him. For the first time in living memory, men of more than one tribe fought alongside each other under Ambrosius' banner, and because of this, the Saxons were pushed back within the boundaries of the lands originally gifted to them by Gwytheryn and kept there, for a time at least. But still they were not driven out of the land.

Ambrosius was no longer young. He had fought with the legions in Gaul, learning his skills from no less a man than the Riothamus Uthyr, before he fell, or vanished, fighting the Parisi. There were a few who began to wonder about a successor, while others who had heard about the coming of the true king fell to wondering how and when he would announce himself.

Ambrosius himself had thought of this question often in the past year, lying awake on his narrow army cot, pondering over all the opportunist king-lets who had left the body of the land torn and bleeding, wondering who would follow him and which of his own men he could put forward when the time came. None, it seemed, could even begin to measure up to the enormity of the task—that of keeping together a kingdom that had been, so often, broken. Long years of army service, followed by more years in the task he had found awaiting him when he returned to Britain—the restoration of Roman order in a land at war with itself—all this had left no time for his own life. There would be no successor of his own blood.

But in the end, the coming of the king happened naturally, though the true story is strange enough.

Ambrosius had his headquarters in the old Roman fort at Isca Silurum, or the City of the Legions, as it was still known. He lived simply enough, like any soldier, adopting none of the pomp and ceremony he might have affected. This frugality brought reluctant approval even from the haters of all things Roman, who chose to remember Ambrosius' British blood at such times and to acknowledge his abilities as a soldier.

So it was that as Ambrosius sat late one night reading over fresh dispatches from the far north, the leather curtain across the door was pushed back, and there came in a figure with eyes more deep and black than the night itself and a face made all of sharp lines and edges and little flesh, and whose voice, when he spoke, was as harsh as a raven's croak.

"Ambrosius Aurelianus, I must have speech with you."

And though he was taken somewhat off guard by the sudden and dramatic appearance of the stranger, Ambrosius answered coolly enough. "Speak, since you are here, but be brief, for as you see, I am busy."

The stranger's face seemed to grow even sharper as he answered. "You have held the land well, Ambrosius, but the time has come for you to relinquish your place to another."

"Who are you?" demanded Ambrosius, calmly enough.

"I am called Myrddin Emrys. I am the Steward of this land."

Now Ambrosius looked with open wonder at the figure before him. The name uttered was one he knew well, for it was already touched with the glow of legend. Few there were who did not know the story of how Gwytheryn, fleeing from Ambrosius' own army, had attempted to build a refuge in the mountains of Eryri, and how each night the work of his builders was thrown down by an unseen agency. It was then that the child Myrddin had come, revealing that two dragons fought beneath the hill, which was sacred to the Goddess of the Land. Subsequently he had prophesied the imminent death of the tyrant, which had proved correct. When his enemies caught up with him at last and burned his camp to the ground, Gwytheryn perished in the flames.

But of the child, Myrddin Emrys, nothing more had been seen of him since that time.

Those events had been little more than eight years since, and then Myrddin had been a child of, perhaps, ten summers; this Myrddin seemed a mature man, yet the more Ambrosius looked at him, the less able he was to put any age upon him.

"Be seated, Myrddin Emrys," he said. "Your name is not unknown to me. But I am unaware of any business you have with me."

"I am but the messenger," replied Myrddin. "The one with whom you must speak is elsewhere."

Ambrosius answered, "Am I to know whom? Indeed, am I to know why I should speak with this person?"

"In time, all will be made plain," was the reply. "For the moment I ask only that you trust me and believe that I mean you no harm."

And Ambrosius, though he might well have done otherwise, nodded his head in assent, and when Myrddin Emrys led the way out into the night, he followed, noting without surprise that they passed through the barracks and into the narrow streets of the town unchallenged by the generally watchful guards.

The sun was a red stain on the horizon as they reached the great amphitheater, pride of Roman Isca, built in the time of the emperor Titus and rising thirty feet above the earth. Its walls were already beginning to crumble into disrepair, and grass and weeds grew tall between broken flagstones and along the stone seats where once citizens and legionaries alike had gathered to watch the games.

So it was that by the light of the setting sun, Ambrosius Aurelianus, *Dux Britanniarum*, came to the center of the great oval space at the middle of the arena and so stood, waiting for he knew not whom or what, wondering, perhaps, why he had allowed himself to be brought there, unarmed, with the evening cold beginning to strike through his cloak and the clothing beneath until he shivered. Of the other, of whom the mage was but a messenger, there was, at first, no sign; while, from the moment they had reached the amphitheater, Myrddin himself had vanished into the shadows. Then, as Ambrosius waited, there came the sound of light footfalls and his soldier's sight identified a dark shape hesitating amid the crumbling stones.

"Come forward!" Ambrosius demanded, more sharply than he had intended. "Show yourself!"

The figure who emerged from the shadows was no fearsome and terrible warrior, no wild monster from the dark Otherworld, but a slight youth of no more than fourteen or fifteen summers, simply dressed and unarmed. When he spoke his voice was light and uncertain.

"My lord?" He spoke in a native dialect familiar to Ambrosius.

"Who are you? What is your name?"

"I have no right to any name until it is won by right."

"Then how shall I call you?"

"My family used to call me Gwri."

Ambrosius found himself smiling. "Very well then. Gwri it shall be. What do you want of me?"

"Something more and something less than your blessing."

"Oh, and what may that be?"

"I have a task to undertake. I must marry the land."

Ambrosius felt his scalp prickle, and an involuntary shudder ran through his body. Though he already knew the answer, he said, "You must explain what you mean."

In formal singsong the youth answered, "I have met the Old One by the stream and have danced her dance. I have drunk of the Red Drink of Lordship and kept vigil at the lip of the well. Still must I play the game of light and dark and seek the cauldron in the four-sided island. But before I do these things, I must ask the word of he who is the Protector of the Island of the Mighty, that when the time comes, I may take his place and stand where he stands."

Ambrosius, every hair on his body standing up, asked, "What word is this that I must give?"

"The word of passing, the word that gives the right to the one who comes after. You must ask the question."

As he heard these words, a strange feeling came upon Ambrosius—that he had heard these self-same words before, and that he knew the answer to the question even before it was out of his mouth. He said, "What are the duties of a king?"

"To love and serve the land."

"What more besides?"

"To be patient; to know self-government without haughtiness; to speak truth and keep promises; to honor the gods, respect poets, and be boundless in charity towards all. To lift up good men and suppress ill-doers; to give freedom to the just, restriction for the guilty. To light a lamp in the minds and hearts of men whom he honors, and to appear as splendid as the sun in his own hall."

The ancient formula sounded familiar to Ambrosius, as though he had always known it. The response came unbidden to his lips. "And when the time comes to lay down your life for the land, what then?"

"Then I shall go willingly to the place where all men must go and drink of the Dark Drink of Forgetting."

As he heard these words, Ambrosius had a strange sensation that more than one voice was speaking—as though a chorus spoke from within the depths of the earth, an endless chain of those who had served the land. And among them, somehow, he also stood, Ambrosius Aurelianus, *Dux Britanniarum*, his native blood calling out from the depth of his being.

The moment passed, as though a shadow had passed over the world. Ambrosius blinked and was once more aware that he stood in the old amphitheater of Caerleon. Before him the boy who had been King Before and would be King Hereafter stood quietly, and for the first time, Ambrosius noticed that where their two shadows slanted away to one side in the light of the sunset, the boy's towered hugely. A kingly shadow, crowned, and with a sword. Ambrosius blinked, and again it seemed that he had imagined what he saw. His eyes met those of the boy, a long and appraising look that spoke of all that he had felt and dreamed and all that was to be. "Will you tell me your true name now?"

"I am called Artorius in the language of the Romans; Artos in our own."

"Artos." He tried the sound of the name. "I believe you will indeed be king after me, perhaps sooner than I had realized. And I believe you may be the one this land has needed and has so long awaited. A dark time is coming for us all, that is certain; it will need great strength to meet it. It seems to me that you have both."

"He has indeed, Ambrosius the Roman." The voice of Myrddin spoke from the shadows, but Ambrosius never took his eyes from those of the young Artos. Wholly caught up in the moment, and with as much ceremony as he knew, he placed his hands on the boy's shoulders.

"You asked for the word that would make the passing of one king and the coming of another happen as it should. Now I can give it. The word is *service*, and you have spoken it already—serve the land and the people who are the land, and they will serve you. Do what must be done, child of the future. Time will do the rest."

Ambrosius turned away and left the amphitheater without looking back. He told no one of what had occurred that night, until he lay dying of poison, introduced by a Saxon spy into the well from which he habitually drank. Then he told the tale to one who was close to him, a young officer named Bedwyr, whose native blood assured him that it would be understood and not forgotten.

That young officer became one of the foremost warriors in the war band of the young king, who became the Ymerawdwr after he drew forth the Glaive of Light from the Stone of Kingship and married the land's Lady. But of that story I will speak no more at this time, for it is a long one and requires more time than I have in this cold place.

F*rom these words I believe this tale to have been set down before its teller Taliesin assumed the office of royal bard to Arthur. In no other place have I read of this fateful meeting, and therefore I believe that Taliesin must have learned it from the lips of either the Ymerawdwr himself or from the ancient one who is named here Myrddin Emrys.*

TALIESIN SINGS OF HIS KNOWLEDGE

Once I knew
everything there was to know;
in a moment of burning ecstasy
I became transformed,
knew every rock and tree
bird, animal and fish;
and, in that moment,
perceived all meanings to be one.

Then, in just as swift a movement
from lightning to returning dark,
I forgot all I had learned,
as though, where once I had beheld
only unities, now I beheld
mere fragmented moieties
which once were whole.

Since then, long years of seeking,
striving to recover the fragments
through which I might, somehow,
put back the broken littoral
into that same whole—an eternity
that does not change—
since then, only I have changed, becoming
somehow frozen in this time.

Now I look back and down
At the past and push

the fragments into new patterns,
hoping still to find
their true relationship—
that the fires of creation,
might once again
be kindled in my bones.

3

THE BRIDE OF THE SPEAR

nce, when I was a young man and scarcely knew of the Wood, I came to a place where no one went, a dread place without light or life. Even then, they called it the Wasted Land, for nothing grew there, and life itself seemed to have fled away. Those who came, in Arthur's time, to know of its true horror have sought to heal it. The high prince Galahad himself came there, as did Llachu, the king's son. I have heard it said that the Wasted Land has indeed been healed, though a part of me believes this cannot ever be so. ❧ Many stories have I heard since then concerning the cause of the blight that lay over the place, and how its effects stretch far beyond the borders—even to the whole of Logres. But when, on a day long ago, I came there, I met with one called the Hag, and from her I heard a story, which I will tell here as I remember it. Whether it is true or not I cannot say, though in my heart I believe it to be a part of the pattern that underlies the history of this land and of the great wood that is Broceliande. Maybe there is no single cause for the Wasteland, and I cannot say with any certainty what the truth is. Yet these are the words of one who perhaps saw the beginning—if not of the Wasteland we have known, then of another. Nor can I say what happened to the one who told this tale to me, for though her last words were of hope, I never saw nor heard of her again.

F*rom my reading of the scrolls, I believe that only rarely did the great bard tell a tale in this fashion. For all that he kept many hundreds of stories and poems in his memory, most often he tells them in his own voice, with all the power of the ancient and terrible knowledge that he possessed. Yet here he allows the voice of another to speak through him. Perhaps it is because this story concerned another harper, not unlike himself, that he chose to do so. Whatever the truth may be, I find this tale strangely more moving than it would have been had it become wholly a part of Taliesin's own story.*

I am of the Clan of the Spear, and I would tell how the destruction known as the Wasted Lands came to be, because of the breaking of a sacred trust and because of the love that I bore for one who was not of the clan and who should never have laid eyes upon that which we guarded.

The valley in which we lived was not like other places. Sickness and death were unknown; the corn grew tall and golden every year; the sun ever shone from a clear sky. This was because of the spear, which stood at the center of the valley, just as the valley stood at the center of the lands beyond. Some say, and I have no means to know otherwise, that while our land burgeoned, so did those that surrounded it.

My father was a proud man who took his duties as Guardian seriously. As Spear King he must not only care for the sacred weapon, but also take part in a yearly ritual, one which also involved my mother, the Spear Queen, and me, the Spear Maiden. We three must together and separately make offerings in the secret way that was ours from the beginning. Every year, at the Feast of the Blessing of the Spear, the king heated the fires of life, brought out the sacred tools of the smith, and in full view of all, remade the head of the spear and fitted it onto the shaft that was always the same, ancient and blackened from generations of handling, the pictures which once adorned it almost rubbed away and no longer readable.

Then, when this was done, the queen and the maiden took the new spear deep into the forest, and at a certain place known only to them, passed from mother to daughter through the ages, the queen ritually anointed the blade with her own blood. When this was done, she would stretch out her arms and offer the spear to the gods above and the gods beneath—and always, a shaft of sun would pierce the canopy of leaves above her and strike the blade until it splintered with light. This done, she would hand the weapon to me, the Spear Maiden, who had come prepared with a bird from the royal dovecotes. This it was my task to dispatch, with the right words and the proper gestures, so that all should be well with the land.

Once, it was said the maiden would have made another kind of offering, after which she was maiden no longer, but rather the Bride of the Spear; earlier even than that, in a time so long past it was scarcely a memory, the king himself would have given up his life for the good of the land. But in the time of which I speak, no such terrible offering had been demanded for many generations, and the land continued to prosper. There was no death, and the corn grew tall in the fields beyond the walls of our village. Each year, after the blessing, the spear was set upright on the hill that overlooked our homes. Garlands were placed upon it, and youths and maidens danced around it so that they, and the land, might be fertile.

And so it was, year upon year, without change—until the day when a stranger came into our lives, who was to change them forever.

It was many years since we had last seen anyone from the outside. Few came near the village, and those who did generally failed to notice our presence and thus passed by. This man was different. He had eyes that noticed things, great and small, with equal care. He moved with the grace of a warrior, yet he carried no weapon, only a harp slung across his back in a doeskin bag. And there was that

THE BRIDE OF THE SPEAR

about him that spoke of long dreaming, of one who was already less than half in the land of men.

I believe I loved him from the first, though such was forbidden to the Spear Maiden. I did my best to be formal and polite when in his company, but I believe that my heart betrayed me whenever he came near. And so the pattern was set that was to lead to sorrow and death and the coming of the Wasted Lands.

It was in the summer that he came, so that it was the better part of a year before the next Blessing of the Spear. It was not our way to turn away those whose steps led them to our doors, and so the stranger, whose name was Lugaid, remained with us, playing and singing songs from the land of men to entertain us in the evenings. He never spoke of his life before, of kith or kin or places he had known. Nor did we seek to probe his past, for such matters were his own business and none other's. Yet sometimes I caught sight of a wistful look in his eyes that caused me to wonder for what he yearned, or why he had come to the Valley of the Spear.

Despite all I could do to prevent it, we were sometimes alone in each other's company, and at such times a silence fell between us that said more than words. Then one day as I walked in the woods, Lugaid's path crossed mine, and in a little while, and with few words, we lay together beneath the trees of the sacred wood. Afterwards, I wept for the shame of what I had done, for surely now that I was maiden no longer, the gods would curse us and the land would wither.

Throughout the year, Lugaid and I continued to meet in the secret depths of the wood. Sweet were those days, and harder it became to keep silent and to hide the terrible secret that was ours. Nor, though we were as close as a man and a woman can be, did I learn anything more about him. His past remained forever undisclosed, as much to me as to the rest of the valley.

Then, as the long chill nights of winter drew upon us, an old woman of the clan died, the first for many generations, and a shiver of fear passed through every one of us. Nursing my secret, part joy, part terror, I blamed myself for the death and for a time refused Lugaid. But the year turned, and as spring drew near, I gave way again to the desire I felt for him, and once more we met whenever we might.

But we grew careless, until at last word reached the king my father, and though I heard afterwards that at first he refused to believe the tale, at length he was driven to follow me, and there he came upon us, Lugaid and I, locked in sweet embrace. With a terrible cry, he leapt upon us with drawn sword.

My lover fled, being unarmed. Fleet of foot and younger than my father, he drew away. Crying I knew not what, I followed them and came to the Hill of the Spear in time to witness a terrible deed. My father had pressed Lugaid to the very place where the spear stood, the ribbons and garlands long since gone from it, its blade tarnished and darkened by wind and weather. I saw without understanding as Lugaid pulled the spear from its resting place and turned it upon my father. The king fell bleeding from a wound in the thigh and, seeing me, cried out in a high and terrible voice to avenge him and the life of the clan.

At such times, a part of the mind that is older than the rest takes charge. I was no longer the lover of the man before me; his face no longer seemed sweet and familiar. I saw only one who had committed a deed of awful sacrilege. I took up the spear from where he had let it fall and struck down the man I had lain with for almost a year with as little thought as I gave to one of the doves I killed in the wood each year.

But already the damage was done. The spear, which was in our sacred keeping, had twice been used to draw blood in a manner not of the rites. Rain began to fall from the moment the king received his wound and kept up its beating for three weeks after, until the corn lay flattened and the land grew sick. Many of the clan fell victim to agues and began to die. The king lay in perpetual agony, his wound unhealing and his manhood dead.

At length the queen, who had scarcely spoken to anyone since that terrible day, gathered those who remained of the clan about her and said: "We must leave this place and take the king to where he may be healed!" And so it was agreed. But when the wagons departed a few days after, with the king's litter in their midst, I did not go with them.

This was my just punishment, that I should remain here alone until such time as one came who could heal the land. I have waited long since then, more years than I can count. Few faces have I seen, and none that stayed to talk with the one whom they call the Hag of the Swamplands.

You are the first who has spoken with me in all that time, so you must not be surprised if I am filled with hope that you may be the one I have waited for these long years. Last night I dreamed of a hill on which stood a house of gold. Before it was planted a new spear, and as I watched, I saw a blackbird settle at its feet and

38

begin to peck at the earth, while from the tip of the spear flew a white dove that mounted into the sky.

C *ould it be that the house of gold described by the old woman in her vision was none other than Camelot the Golden, the great citadel of Arthur, which was yet to be built in the time of which the bard speaks? I have often wondered if this might be so, just as I wonder if the mysterious woman found rest in the end.*

TALIESIN IN WINTER

*Under the ridged brow of winter
the poet hunched, staring out
from the black branches
of the starving wood,
his breath a white fog
from which words formed:*

*"Goddess of the cold and ice
I surrender to your touch,
melting down to darkness
under the hard earth—
where stars still shine,
and where, in the breath between
one winter and the next,
I find a message written.*

*"No words," he sang, "can cause
such truths to pour forth,
drawn from the edge of winter
into the open hand of day.*

39

"Only my faith in the coming
of signs in the dreaming place
confirms in me the knowledge
of winter's flint words."

Sent forth, the poet danced,
left bird prints in the white
unvarying snowfields where
he found clear answers
not even he could share.

4

IN THE PRISON OF
ARIANRHOD

hree times have I been in the prison of Arianrhod, and each time I have seen things that changed me forever. Not that I sought these things, but they sought me. Certainly the prison of which I speak may be understood in many ways. In the everyday human world, it has no existence. Yet sometimes it appears, briefly, on the horizons of our sight, and when it does, we are drawn to it. It is a place of forgetting and of remembering. It is the prison of truth, where what must be spoken is spoken, where nothing may be held back no matter what happens because of it. Perhaps, at the last, it will be my home. ❧ As for Arianrhod herself, who can truly say what she is? ❧ "Goddess," some call her; "nemesis," she is to others. In the cold chambers of my heart, she shines forth like the stars themselves—the very stars over which she is said to hold sway. I came to her, in other times, in search of the knowledge and wisdom that surpasses all other. I stood before the great mirror that is hung in the highest chamber of her tower, and there I saw things that no man may speak of, not even I. Among

those of which I may speak, I saw once the reason for my having drunk of the cauldron of knowledge. There, also, I saw the passing of the king's son into the place that is beyond all knowledge.

But how can one ever know with certainty when a thing is true? In all my dealings with the folk of the Sidhe, in all my long years of service to the Wood, of service to Arthur, there have been events I could not explain. I no longer desire to know the reason for these things; yet I continue to wonder, to scratch at the surface of those darker matters that haunt me still.

Sometimes I would dream, or seem to dream, adrift in the spaces between the worlds at the heart of Arianrhod's domain. There, I heard words, patterns of story that followed me in my waking hours until I set them down or spoke them aloud in the halls of kings. One such story tells of a prisoner who came out of the darkness and into the light to discover that his life was changed forever. Two names I thought I heard—in that part of my mind that is behind and beneath all other ways of thought. One was Elcmar and the other Oengus. My sense of them was brief, a vision that took me deeper into that place that is both outside and within this world than ever before. I was, briefly, in the mind of the prisoner, feeling what he felt, hearing what he heard, knowing what could not be expressed and scarcely named. And I knew him to be caught, within and beneath the land where She Who Is the Land lies waiting for us all, as once she waited for my lord Arthur himself, and will wait for him again at the end of his days. In a part of myself that does not care to admit these things, I knew that my own fate was linked with these things in a similar way. Though I have known no imprisonment such as this man knew, yet I am myself forever caught within the entangling branches of the Wood, eternally part of the story of this land.

Not all the tales that were collected by my ancient brother concerned the life or time of the great bard—though I believe that somehow they reflected the deep inner life which continued within him always. This story seems to me to be of a different kind from all the rest. I must confess that, while I scarcely understand its meaning, it has continued to haunt me since I first read it. Here I seem to sense something of a pain that ran very deep and was as much to do with the bard's own life as with those of whom he wrote.

In the darkness of the mound he began to think, to remember. Turn back the wheel. The stars flowing back. The clouds coiling backward across a slate sky. The last glimmer of light vanishing as the stone rolled across.

He halted this train of thought, shifted himself to ease the throbbing in his right thigh, settled back, easing one hip into a hollow in the earth. Earth. He listened. Felt the slow, steady rhythm of breath. His own? Hers? Quietly he drew a breath of clear air—it would be many days, nights (meaningless terms) before he no longer needed breath. He allowed the images to rise, slowly at first, then quickly, until the hot torrent of memory overwhelmed him and he slipped away from the darkness and was himself again, in sunlight, under a pale, blue-washed sky.

Running, laughter in his throat and wind tugging his hair. But hard though he ran, there was no overtaking her. Boand. The flash of her body, far ahead now, topping the rise, vanishing amid trees. He slowed, no longer racing, pulling air into his lungs in grateful gulps. Memory within memory, of Boand, in her green dress, smiling as she emerged from the door of her father's house. Memory—the trees enclosing him, the path only a shadow in thick leaf mold. She must be far ahead now, unless she had waited? Was that a movement ahead, between the trees? The leaves shivered as though stirred by a breath of wind; but there was none. It was in his mind to call out to her, but he knew this was not part of the pattern he had entered when he began. He saw for a moment the face of the priest, hand raised in blessing, and the dark motion of Boand speeding away.

He came into the place where the leaves had moved and found no one. Softly now, he went forward. Somewhere near she was, for he could sense her presence. The trees ahead thinned suddenly, and he found himself standing in a glade. On all sides great smooth trunks towered skyward—a brief flash of blue where they ended. Ahead, where the trees closed in again, he saw a long, low building, little more than a green mound. Momentarily, he was puzzled. He knew this place, knew the trees. Yet there was no clearing, no hut. Yet, they were here.

He went forward, unconsciously dropping into a hunting crouch. Closer, too, the mound resolved itself into a bothy, the turf hut roughly oval in shape, roofed with green turf, eves overhung so far that there was scarcely a handspan between them and the earth. At the end closest to him was an entrance, no more than a gap in the wall, black and somehow forbidding. He paused before it, ears stretched for sounds of movement from within. He thought he heard something. Moved closer. Stepped within.

In the mound that was now all his world, he was again aware of the cold ground, the still sharp, though retreating, fire in his leg. He closed his eyes, squeezing them tight until the colored shapes danced beneath his lids. He laughed softly, a surprising sound in that place. What use to close the eyes when, open or shut, there was only darkness? He shifted again, moving softly until the space beneath the mound was replaced by the space within the bothy—if, indeed, there was any difference.

He sensed movement. This time he framed her name: Boand. No reply, but a definite sense of movement now, as though someone had moved away from him, retreating into the darkest recesses of the room. He glanced behind him; the door was outlined in dim tree light, green and cool. He felt uneasy with the prickling of an unfamiliar place. He sniffed, breathing in the smells: earth mostly, and peat, his own sweat, and something else. A woman smell.

Gingerly, he took a step, hands before him like a blind man. There began to be born upon him an image, spreading in his mind as though someone had struck an actual light. This strange illumination revealed to him a shape ahead of him in the low-roofed hut. A woman shape: dark hair, delicate limbs. Boand. Yet not Boand. But then, who? His senses swam, as if he were inhaling smoke or strong perfume. His heart began to race, and he felt rising heat suffuse his loins. Despite himself, he trembled. This could not be Boand; this was no girl. Yet it was she. He

THE PRISONER OF ARIANHROD

could, with what sight had been vouchsafed to him, "see" her: the pale, narrow face, framed in black hair; the slender body he had last glimpsed fleeing before him through the trees.

He found it strangely hard to move; yet he knew he must. He advanced a step, and with that seemed to see more clearly. A gleam of pale flesh. Lust stirred in him. But such lust! Such a flood of hunger that, had it struck him in daylight, in his own place, could have meant only one thing. Here, he seemed held by the power as it mounted within him. His movements were as slow as a dreamer, as though he were suspended in liquid and could not impel himself forward any faster. He tried to focus his attention on the woman in front of him, on the gracefully rounded curves half-visible in the dim light.

It seemed an age before he reached her, stumbling suddenly to his knees at her side, almost flung upon her by the sudden releasing of his body from whatever had held him. Now that she was near, he felt suddenly afraid of touching her. Her face and body were Boand's, yet she was a stranger to him in a way that he could not comprehend. He felt her eyes upon him, and with that, a shock ran through his body that left him gasping. He felt life spilling from him like blood, and he shuddered with the force of it—yet he was withdrawn, far away, detached, as though it were happening to another. Normally he would have felt shamed, but not now. And he saw that she-who-was-Boand was smiling at him, had raised a hand first to her lips, then to his brow, where she placed her fingers for a moment.

Immediately it was as though he had woken from a long sleep. He saw clearly. The face of the woman was close to him. He felt her breath on his cheek. In clarity of action, he moved toward her. As though from a great height he saw himself, far below, cover the woman's body with his own. He seemed a giant, standing hugely astride the land, and in some way that he could scarcely comprehend, the woman was the land: her rich limbs and mounded breasts the hills and valleys, combes and vales. Vast forms moved across his vision, and he was part of them, moving to their rhythm and their time, infinitely slower than his own. In ecstasy, he felt a hot unquenchable fire in his body that seemed to come from far beneath him. For a moment he was both far above and present in his own body, and with that came the sense that he was driving deep into the earth.

With a shock of pain and a cry that echoed in his mind as it must have echoed across the land, he came fully awake, found himself standing with face and body pressed hard against a damp wall of earth—the wall of the mound. Rivulets of sweat burst from him and flowed over his breast and thighs. He tasted salt on his lips, and it stung his eyes. He felt that he was being pressed downward into the earth itself, compressed into a ball of clay. And with the feeling, strangely, came another. A sense of being expelled, of coming forth from sleep, or a dark place, or a long dream. In the silence that eternally filled the mound, he felt the surge and flux of a great roaring sound, like a river that had burst its banks and then rushed away in a great flood, leaving its bed empty and dry. So he felt also, and the darkness that had been not empty before, now seemed chill and barren.

For a timeless time he stood thus, trying to remember if this were the mound or the turf hut into which he had crawled long since. How long? Or whether they were one and the same. Tried to remember the face of the woman, of Boand. The words of the priest came back to him, and with them, the touch of her hand on his brow: *You shall know the wisdom of she who bore us, and you shall have congress with her and of the twain shall be born the child who sanctifies the land.* Like an echo in his mind the thought ran, and he felt cold, alone, spent.

Slowly he sank down in that lightless place and eased himself into a position so that his back was against the wall. Sighing, he leaned his head back and stared with sightless eyes towards where the roof must stretch. There, he saw what at first he thought was the illusion of lights: minute pinpricks piercing the darkness. He blinked his eyes, thinking these were lights he saw when he pressed his fingers upon his closed lids. But his eyes were open, and the darkness was less dark above him. For a long time he sat still, until the pattern asserted itself into a dimly recognizable form. Stars. Sky. The roof of the world and the roof of the mound.

Then a voice boomed out of the darkness, a voice so vast that it must come from beyond those tiny points of light. It was a single word, a name, repeated over and over, at first without meaning but gradually coming clearer. A name— *Elcmar.* A name dimly familiar. His own name. With a cry he leapt up towards that voice, his own raised in feeble answer. The mound opened above him, breaking open like the membrane of an egg, and he burst upwards into light. Such light as he had never known or could have guessed at. The great voice slid into silence, leaving him alone. He stood upon a great plain, stretching upon all sides. Above him the sun glared like a golden beetle and coming towards him . . .

I must confess that I know not whether what follows here is a part of the same vision of which the great bard spoke, or some other. All that I can say is that the scrolls on which these lines were written were of a kind, and the writing, camped and spidery as all those written, I believe, by Taliesin himself, seemed to be the same.

His name was Oengus and he was always trying to remember who had given it to him. In the distance, he remembered that he had once been called names like *Young* and *Son*. In the distance, memory occluded. He was always trying to remember something. Images of a breaking flood, a great plain, the high round orb of the sun. And under it, within it, in the midst, a face, seamed and wrinkled like the earth, with a wide lipless mouth opening to speak . . .

What words he could never tell, only that they were important to him, as important as a name, the most secret and powerful thing any one person could know about another. In his own name, he somehow knew, was a great mystery that would open doors, cause mounds to gape, turn rivers in their beds. But he knew nothing of its meaning and did not dare to ask. Afraid of the answers and what they might mean. All quests began that way, he knew, and it was not long before he realized that he was already embarked upon just such a one.

The days dawned, indeed, when he found himself walking away from the place that had always been home, without a thought for where it would lead, where he was heading. He crossed the wide flat plain and came to the edge of the hills. Beyond them, he caught a glimpse of trees. He walked through the wood, drank in its scents, and watched its changing patterns. All day he walked until the trees were left behind, and he came to a place where the hills shouldered up from the earth, cracking it open and rising upward.

Finally he came to an opening in the hillside: a cave mouth opening into darkness. As he had been taught, he entered without hesitation, raising his hand before him and speaking aloud the words he had learned long since but never, until that day, spoken. The darkness of the place ebbed before him, and he stared about in the soft gleam of a light. The wall of the place told a story of habitation from the first palm print to the last leaping stag. Here must be the secret, the thing he sought. He sat down in the center of the strange rock world and set himself to remembering all that he saw. It took a while, and when he was at last familiar with every mark on the walls of the cave, he felt tired. Dousing the light, he walked outside, drawing strength as always from the warmth of the sun's rays. Then he lay down upon the warm stones and closed his eyes in sleep.

Dreams came at once, and once again he saw the great face rising above him, speaking great words that filled his mind and fell like invisible fire around him. Then he was suddenly awake in a strange place filled with light that seemed to magnify everything upon which it fell. Under its radiance, the earth was a map of cracks and crevices, each of which seemed to tell a story: what had once been there, who had come and who had passed, a chain of memories binding him to that place as though it had been his for all time.

Unbidden, then, came the memory, the scent of a white flower that made everything else seem like a wilderness—but it was not. Stars shone, and grass grew here, under the high bright glow. And with the knowledge of the flower came another kind of knowing—that under the guise of stem and petals lay a form sleeping—a bright stepping form in which the legend of spring was reborn, moment to moment in the tears of winter.

On his bed of stone the sleeper turned, restless as a bird before the onset of storms; with his turning, the dream turned, and from the images within the cave came further knowledge: He stood at the entrance to a grove, deep-wooded, held in stillness like a breath of sunlight. In his hands was a harp, and though in the world from which he came, waking, he knew nothing of the art of music, here he drew from its strings such vibrations of sound that the very wind wept, and the trees bowed before him their deep rustling valances.

But she moved not, nor breathed but lightly, where she stood, white as swan's feathers at the distant end of the grove. Caught in arrested movement, like a deer in flight or a bird about to take wing, she turned an eye brighter than moonlight upon him, and the harp quaked and grew still in his hands. With great sweeps of light, flashing like paddles in sunlit water, she grew feathered and beaked and swam in the air with great pinions of snow, so that he, too, must follow her as a brown hawk spinning in silver shadow. Driven by desire, his raptor's cry rang out in the shadow of the sun. Long and long their racing wings beat sparks from the anvil of air before her song broke free and all time stilled to hear it.

Restless again, he turned on his pillow of polished stone and stood again upon the bruised earth, which cried out for the passing of her love. Enraged, like a winter storm, he wept, and finding again the harp in his two hands, he fought the season to an end and brought the sun back from beneath the world as a gift for her. Sailing on wings of spun silver, the swan entered his dream, and where her feet touched, the earth sprang open and white flowers bloomed.

Waking, the dreamer sprang from his couch of stone and fled back down the hillsides and through the trees, on into the silence of the white lands until the green mound of his home swam into vision. Crying aloud—his words like a swan's silver singing or a harsh hawk's cry—he broke open the crusted wards of memory, saw again the retreating waters, the white hills opening and the blue glass sky overhead. In his ears a cry rang forth, and his name became to him a sword. Standing still on the top of the green mound, he sought the strings of the harp and sang season through season until his joy was spent and the small flame of life burned steadily at his feet. Then he stepped down, sure now in the knowledge of himself, and took the hand that was stretched out to him and went into the green mound. And there he stayed long in the shadow of the sun and the purity of the rain and the blessing of the earth until their joy fruited into life.

In darkness, I heard these words, saw these things, and with the part of my mind that continues to ask questions, to fit together the pieces, to seek a pattern in the fragments of the whole, I thought that in this ancient tale I heard echoes of my own life. Had the one named Elcmar come to the mound of forgetting, a place where sacrifice and the marriage of man with the earth took place? Or was he, who sought for his name and an understanding of his role in the world, the offspring of another such wild mating? In all truth, I cannot say.

Once, kings married the land, as Arthur married Gwenhwyfar. But these men of whom I've written here were of a more ancient time, a time before time itself as we know it. Perhaps Arianrhod sought to show me these things so that I might better understand my own place in the patterns of Arthur's world. I do not know. Yet, in my heart, I still feel the beat of the earth as it resounded in Elcmar's blood and, as I look up to the sun, I remember the one named Oengus coming forth into the day.

THE SALMON OF WISDOM

I walked in the silent Wood,
Where sunlight struck deep
Like a sword between the trees.
Halting by a river-fed pool,
I murmured: "Salmon of Wisdom,
Today I saw one walking
Whose breath became my breath,
Whose hand brushed mine
Like a fiery kiss, who left
A trail of stars
In the glitter of the grass.
Who, when I looked, wore on her brows
A jewel of undying light."

Looking into the water, I saw
A speckled body drift
Into the stream that carried it away.
In its own time it would answer—
Meanwhile, there were songs to find!

Part II
BARDIC TALES

THE ISLAND OF SORROW AND JOY

5
THE ISLAND OF
SORROW AND JOY

I have spoken before of the Wastelands: of how, before the time of Arthur, there came into being a place where nothing would grow—where no seeds sprouted and no fresh leaves grew on the trees; where rivers ran dry and streambeds were cracked and empty. Many tales are told of how this came to be and how it ended. She who called herself the Bride of the Spear told me how she brought the curse upon the land through her love for a wandering harper. Another tale says that the land was laid waste because of the theft of a sacred thing, long kept by the dwellers in Avalon, an act that brought devastation in its wake. Still others call that thing the Grail—though I would say it was not so—and speak of how its passage through the land at that time brought about not only the Wastelands but also, perhaps, their cure. But I have heard another tale, and I will tell it here, since it is part of the song of the Great Wood, where I found my own roots.

*gain and again the great bard speaks of the Wood, and from his own words
and those of the little monk who was the first collector of these tales, I
have learned that it was far more than a simple stretch of trees of which he spoke.
Even in the seclusion of Ynys Witrin I have heard whispers of Broceliande, the forest
that once covered most of Britain. Long ago it was destroyed, or simply faded from
the knowledge of humankind, yet men still speak of it in whispers and make the sign
of the horns against ill luck when they do so. I must confess that I do not truly
understand these matters, yet I believe that when he speaks of the Wood, the bard
speaks not of any place but of a state of being, such as the Blessed Saints themselves
aspire to.*

There were two brothers, and their names were Bran and Sgeolan. They
eked out a living as fishermen on an inhospitable coast of the Island of the Mighty,
and though it was a hard life, it was less so than formerly, before the Irish raiders
were driven away by the warriors of Arthur. So the brothers were content enough,
until there came upon them events that were to change them both forever and
change the history of the Island of the Mighty.

This was the way of it. One morning, at the end of summer, there came a
knock at the door of the bothy where Bran and Sgeolan dwelled. Opening the
door, Bran saw a figure muffled deeply against the cold, who, when it spoke, had
a woman's voice. That surprised Bran as much as anything, for it was not often in
those times that one saw a woman unattended, especially not one who spoke like
a noble. But he bade her come in to the fire, and when she pushed back the hood
of her cloak, he saw that she had a fine pale face with great dark eyes in it and a
look upon her of one that had come far with little food and less shelter.

So Bran got her some bread and some of the soup from the cauldron that
hung by the fire. When some of the pinched look had gone from her face, he
asked her politely enough what had brought her to that lonely place.

She said, "You and your brother are fishermen. You have a boat. I would take
passage with you."

Bran was so surprised at this, and at the strange way the woman talked, that he quite forgot to notice that she knew he had a brother, though Sgeolan was at that moment away working at the nets down by the shore. But he nodded anyway and said cautiously, "Where might you wish to go, lady?"

"To the island," said she, and Bran grew pale as she spoke, for though there were many islands off the coast, yet he knew somehow that she meant but one of them, and that one had a grim history that kept most men away from its shores. When he made no answer, the woman spoke again. "I must get across to the island. You are the only ones who can take me. Please!"

"I must ask my brother," said Bran.

The woman sat still. "He is coming," she said.

"Ask him now."

And before Bran could say more, the door opened, and Sgeolan came in with a gust of chill air, beating his hands against his sides to warm them. He stopped in surprise when he saw the woman and looked inquisitively at his brother.

"This lady wishes us to take her to the island," said Bran carefully. "What is your word, brother?"

Sgeolan said, "That is something I would not wish to do."

The woman said again,

"Please!" with such desperation in her that Bran and Sgeolan looked at each other. When Sgeolan shrugged, Bran said, "Very well. We will take you. But do not expect us to wait for you."

"That you will not need to do."

"Then let us go," said Bran and took his tattered cloak from where it hung by the door.

The woman did not speak again as they walked the short distance to the shore. Bran and Sgeolan pushed their small craft into the sea and helped her aboard. The woman remained silent as they pulled away from the shore. Once out of the shelter of the land, the water was rough, a strong swell running before an easterly wind; but Sgeolan plied the oars steadily, and Bran steered the craft with a firm hand on the sweep, while the woman sat in the prow and stared forward as though she was hungry to see their destination.

It was not a long journey to the island, but the weather worsened steadily as they drew near. Soon they could see the shoreline, and grim and forbidding it seemed, as was always the case to those who looked upon it from the direction of the land. Bran and Sgeolan had lived within sight of the place for many a year, and its outlines were familiar. Yet they never looked that way without a shiver of fear, for it was said that the island was a place of spirits and wonders, where perhaps the old gods themselves still lived—even Bendegeid Vran himself, whose name the fisherman bore. And more than once they had seen strange lights on that distant shore, before hastening to look away and make the sign of the horns against evil.

Yet now, as they neared a line of rocks, against which the waves beat thunderously, Bran suddenly pointed ahead with a shaking hand. When Sgeolan paused in his rowing and looked over his shoulder, he gave a gasp of fear. The whole island seemed wrapped in a ghostly shawl of light, as though a curtain stretched between the place where their frail craft rode the churning sea and the shore of the island. There, where none had been before now, they saw the outline of a small stone chapel. From its narrow door and even narrower window spilled light of such intensity that it seemed as though the sun was rising within.

Yet, though the brothers were shaken by what they saw, they did not hesitate for more than a moment. Sgeolan began to row as though his life depended upon it, while Bran clung to the sweep for dear life. Only their silent passenger showed neither fear nor astonishment but clung to the sides of the craft with both hands.

Then, when it seemed the craft must be dashed to pieces against the cliffs of the island, the wind dropped and the sea became flat calm—calm as it seldom was along that bleak and barren coast. Sgeolan sculled into the lea of the island, and the brothers beached their craft easily on a shelving lip of sand. Bran helped their passenger on to dry land and was about to push the boat off again and leap back aboard when his eyes caught those of his brother. Sgeolan was staring fixedly at something behind him. Fearful of what he might see, Bran turned to look, but there was nothing there except a narrow path that climbed inland and the smooth sand that stretched away on either hand. The woman had already vanished from sight, having not even waited to speak her farewells.

Bran turned back to Sgeolan with a question on his lips, but before he could ask it, his brother stood up, leaped ashore, and without a word began to hurry inland. Bran called his name to no avail, and when he received no answer, followed him, all the while looking over his shoulder and to either side in apprehension of what he might see.

The climb was easier than it seemed, and in no time Bran stood for the first time on the summit of the isle and looked across towards the mainland. What he saw there caused him to stare. A dark cloud seemed to hang over the Island of the Mighty, but it was no ordinary cloud such as might bring stinging rain or battering winds. This was a deep midnight smirch, rank and bitter as the smoke of burning thatch, and it seemed as impenetrable as a shield of ancient power.

Terror overcame Bran, and he turned about and called out to his brother. But there was no sign of Sgeolan or of the woman. Both vanished as though the earth had swallowed them, although there were neither trees nor rocks to shield them from sight, only the narrow stone cell that they had seen from the water and that now no longer gave off a brilliant light. Then Bran saw that away to his right lay a small huddle of buildings, built like beehives around a taller structure of the same shape. There Bran could see figures moving, and though his teeth rattled in his head with fear of the place, he would not depart until he had found Sgeolan. So, he turned that way and hastened towards the buildings as swiftly as he might.

As he neared the little collection of huts, he heard singing, and then he saw a strange procession coming towards him. In the front came several men in white garments who carried tall candlesticks and sang as they walked. Behind them came others carrying a litter on their shoulders, on which lay a woman deathly pale and thin, covered in heavy drapes against the cold. By her side walked the woman whom Bran and Sgeolan had ferried to the island. She had taken off her cloak, and Bran saw that she was clothed like a princess with gold at wrist and throat. At the end of the procession came several simply dressed men and women, and among them was his brother.

"Sgeolan," he cried and hurried to his side. Sgeolan beamed at him but laid a finger to his lips.

As Bran joined him, Sgeolan leaned close and said softly, "We go to heal the Queen." Bran stared at him in bewilderment and was about to ask what he meant and to tell him to come away, when Sgeolan laid a finger again to his lips and taking Bran's arm, pulled him into step with the rest. For a moment, Bran thought of pulling his brother physically away and back to the boat, but then something, curiosity perhaps, made him pause. For all their strangeness, these folk seemed to mean them no harm. With some reluctance, he allowed himself to be borne along with the procession, which he saw was making for the chapel.

As they drew near, light once again burst from within, and the singers fell silent as though at a signal. Then the front of the procession passed through the doors, and the woman on the litter was carried within, the other walking still at her side. The chapel was small, and the rest of the party, including Bran and Sgeolan, had to remain outside. By craning forward, they could just see inside, and Bran looked with curiosity to see what was happening. Afterwards he was never quite sure of what he saw, and though he told the tale many times, he never really understood it. I tell it merely as it has come down to me, without comment, though I have heard many different reasons for what took place.

As he looked into the small chapel, Bran saw that the woman in the litter had been laid before a rough hewn altar stone on which had been set a cup that blazed with a light so bright that he could not look at it directly. Also present was the woman they had brought from the mainland, seated in a great, carved, wooden chair, like a throne. By her side stood a man in rich robes, embroidered with wondrous designs in many colors. The white robed ones were ranged upon either side.

Then, as Bran watched, the richly robed man standing by the altar took up the cup of light, which somewhat modified its glow, and in the other hand, a little silver knife. The woman on the throne held out her arm, bare from the shoulder. The little knife flashed once, and red drops of blood began to flow from the woman's arm into the cup. Though she made no sound or sign of pain, Bran saw that she grew paler at every moment, and her dark eyes seemed to grow ever larger.

At length the cup seemed to be filled, and the man in the rich robes bent over the body of the woman in the litter and, raising her up, seemed to offer the cup to her. Bran remained forever unsure of the order of events, which seemed to merge into one another. He recalled the woman rising from her litter and that she seemed younger than before, though perhaps it was only that she was in some way healed. And he remembered that the other, she who had but lately sailed with them, had slipped quietly into the great chair, and that her eyes were closed.

Then things became even more confused as he stood aside and watched the newly healed woman emerge with the cup in her hands and, walking to the edge of the cliffs, empty what it contained into the sea. It seemed that he also heard words, though what they were he would never recall: something about the Wasteland and the sovereignty of the Island of the Mighty. Then the whole group began to wend its way back as they had come, leaving Bran and Sgeolan standing alone on the rocky headland beside the chapel. Later Bran told how, when he looked once more within, he could see no sign of the woman who had occupied the great chair and that the light was gone from the altar.

After that, the two brothers hastened back to the shore and sailed back across the strait, which was now peaceful and calm. Nor did they speak at all until they were safely home and seated together inside the bothy with the fire banked and platters of steaming food before them.

Then Bran looked across at his brother and asked the question he had most need to ask. "Why did you follow her, brother?"

And Sgeolan looked back with wrinkled brow and said, "Because she was the Queen."

Whether he meant the woman in the litter or their passenger, Bran could never discover, for Sgeolan refused to talk of the event again. But it is told that after this happening, the two men could not settle to their old way of life, but became wanderers through the land, until in time they came to the court of the Ymerawdwr Arthur and took service with him.

There they learned of the days, not long past, when a terrible blight lay upon the land, when the king himself fell sick and the queen journeyed far from the court in search of a remedy for his malaise. For long months she remained absent. Then one day the people heard birds singing where they had been too long silent, and when they looked out of their houses, they saw the first green of spring upon the trees and in the fields. That day the queen returned, and it was soon known that the Ymerawdwr was well again, so that there was much rejoicing throughout the land.

And whether it is to be believed that the queen was indeed she whom Bran and Sgeolan saw lying sick unto death in the Island of Sorrow and Joy, or whether it was she whom they carried to the island, I shall not say at this time. But it is said that the brothers became great warriors in the service of the emperor and were known by other names in the tales that are told of those times. But when first they came into the presence of the Lord and Lady of the land, the queen leant forward and smiled at them and said, merely, "Welcome."

There is a mystery in this tale that I cannot fathom. I have heard tell how in that far-off time when Arthur was king or emperor in these lands that he did indeed fall sick, and that in some way he was healed—though how this came about no one speaks any more. When I read these words I seem to become aware of something that I cannot explain, as though the very words grew bright with meaning, and I saw what they described in a part of myself that is neither mind nor heart.

Could it be that the cup of which the bard writes was that very cup with which Our Lord Jesu celebrated the first Eucharist? Other tales that I found among the ancient scrolls suggest that this may be so. For myself, I do not know, though I continue to wonder at the mystery that is here.

TALIESIN TO THE CROWS

First in autumn,
through spring
into summer—
mix-matched seasons
and only winter left—
I came adrift
in a sea of memory
and sank
in a sudden chill
that swept the waves.

Borne under
I lay in the deep,
bosomed in peace,
where only the
sound of singing
pierced
the waves' sad thunder.

And now, at rest
(they say),
I turn and master
the tides that flow
over and under,
over and under
this deep delved hollow
filled with late blooming fire—

that slow, sad harvest,
pressed by necessity,
into the shape
of a winter dream.

6

LUGH OF THE STRONG ARM AND THE THREE QUEENS

here are so many stories about Ancel, or Lancelot as I have heard him called of late, but few know that once he had another name and that he is remembered by the bards of the Island of the Mighty as Lugh of the Strong Arm. The story I have to tell concerns a time before he became one of Arthur's men and the greatest champion and most feared warrior of all that company. But even then he had the kind of face that drew the attention of women and led him into adventures from which only the strength of his sword arm drew him whole. ❧ On this occasion of which I speak, the hero had gone hunting alone, and such was his success that by noon, he had enough meat to fill even the Cauldron of Dwrnach the Giant for more nights than one. Now in the heat of the day, there came upon him a great desire for sleep, for he had hunted well and come far from his home. And so, having stacked his hunting spears carefully against the bole of a great tree, Lugh cast himself down in its shade and fell into a light sleep—though always his hand lay near to his sword, and he twitched in his sleep like a hound before the fire.

While he lay thus, there was a movement in the forest, and there came into view as strange a procession as any you might see in that time and place. First there came a dwarf carrying a great spear on which was set a freshly severed head—the mouth still gaped in its death shout, and blood darkened the shaft of the spear. Behind this came four ill-shaped creatures, dressed in skins, who seemed as though they had once been tall men, but who now shambled and dragged themselves along like broken beasts. Above them they supported a canopy of rich cloth, finer than anything seen in those parts, and beneath its shade, sitting upon three white ponies, with saddle cloths of softest sheepskin, were three women of such beauty you would have thought they came from the Underland itself. They were dressed in such richness as might have shamed the court of Melwas, King of the Summer Country.

Now when these three saw where Lugh of the Strong Arm lay beneath the tree, they stopped, and seeing how his hand lay close to his broad hafted sword and how his spears stood close at hand, one of them raised her hand and drew upon the air a sign that caused the hero at once to fall into a sleep from which none could have wakened him, save she who cast it.

Then the three got down from their mounts and came nearer. When they looked upon the sleeping youth and remarked upon his beauty and the play of his muscles beneath his breathing skin, they at once fell to arguing. For, said she who had laid the sleep-without-dreams upon him, this was surely the most beautiful creature she had seen this long while, and he must surely be intended for her. She had hair the color of a raven's wing and secret eyes, and her mouth was the color of rowan berries, and her form was fair. Her name was Morgana, though in those days she was not so well-known in the Lowlands as she is now.

Her sisters, who were called Morgause and Argante, were equally fair. The first had hair like a sunset and the second like a bright golden net; and they were all three touched with the gleam of twilight and the radiance of inner earth. And when they looked upon Lugh where he lay, they all three cast lustful thoughts upon him and began to dispute with each other—for it seemed to them that all might have sport with this young hero; but as to who should have him first, they could not agree.

And so at last Morgana, who was the eldest, said, "Let us take him to a safer place than this and, when he wakes, let him decide which of us three he shall sport with first." And by their arts—for they were indeed of elvish stock and well versed in the magic arts—they went from that place to another, deeper in the wards of the ancient Wood, taking the sleeping hero with them. When he woke at last, stretching and turning like one who has slept overlong, he found that he was in a place where branches of hawthorn met over him, and a barrier of thorns was on every side, so that he was as much a prisoner as if he had been held in a room of stone.

Further, he saw that his weapons had all been taken from him while he slept, but that food—barley cakes and a bowl of beer—had been left by his side. And though he knew the prohibition against eating the food of faery—which place this might well be—he was young enough to put the needs of the belly before thought of danger, so he ate and drank his fill and then sat down upon the ground and drew his knees up to his chin and waited for what would occur.

And what did occur was this: There came a high, clear, far-off seeming voice that said words that Lugh could neither hear nor understand—except that they made the hairs on his neck stand up, while a shiver ran through him like one who sees his own grave. Then there came into his prison—how he could not see, since there seemed no entrance or exit—three beautiful women (for such, at least, he supposed them to be) who stood close together as though they were each part of a whole and looked at him. Then Morgana—though he did not know it was she—said, "You are called Lugh of the Strong Arm, and you will be the greatest warrior ever to walk in the halls of the Lord Arthur."

Now these words meant nothing to Lugh, since the name of Arthur was still unknown at that time. He stood up slowly and looked at the three women in the eyes as unflinchingly as he could, though he could not help a small gleed of fear that needed little to fan it into flame. "As to that," he said, "you seem to know well enough who I am; but I would know who it is that has brought me here."

THE THREE QUEENS

"We are the queens of the north and of the south and of the east," said Morgause, "and we have brought you here so that you might choose which of us you will have for your lover."

"Well," Lugh replied, "if I have a choice, I might refuse you all."

The three queens drew even closer together, and it seemed for a moment that Lugh saw before him a great serpent whose scales shone green in the strange light of that place, and it hissed and spat at him. Then Argante, she of the hair like a spun-gold net, spoke up for the first time, "Listen well, warrior," she said, "it would be easy for us to compel you to our need, but it is our will that you choose one of us to lie with. Therefore we shall leave you to think upon this, since we understand that it is no easy thing for any mortal to choose from three such as we. But we shall return shortly, and you must choose by then."

Before Lugh could protest further, he found that he was alone, though the manner of the three women's exit he still could not guess. Then he fell to thinking, and he seemed to remember the four broken creatures who had carried the canopy above the three, and in his mind, he understood that such would be his own fate if he took any one of the queens to his bed. For though he was young and lusty enough to feel desire for all three, he knew also that to love such as they brought only pain and fretful longings. Then in that place of thorns and dim, unfocused light, he knew a great longing to feel the air of the outside world upon his face and to see the sun again. His spirit felt heavy and chill, and he chafed to hold a sword in his hand with which to cut his way out of that place.

Then he heard a voice that spoke to him from beyond the imprisoning hedge and asked him how he fared. "Not well," he answered, "nor is it likely to get any better."

At that there was an audible sigh and a small hole appeared in the spiked thickness of the hedge, and through the hole came a slim white arm and hand, offering a dish of food and a vessel of beer.

Lugh took these and said, "Who is it that asks after my well-being?"

"A prisoner, like yourself."

"And have you a name, fellow prisoner?"

"I had one once, but it is easy to forget."

"Then do you know where this place is?"

"Oh, yes. It is nowhere and everywhere and somewhere."

"That is no answer."

But the arm and hand withdrew and at once the hole closed up, leaving Lugh alone once more. He ate and drank and walked around the confines of the hedge and tried to see what lay beyond it; but where there were chinks in the living wall of his prison, there was only uniform grayness; and save for the sound of his own breathing, there was only silence.

In that place time had no dimension, so that Lugh had no way of telling how long he remained there. Twice more the three queens came to visit him, and each time he refused them. Once, they showed him pictures in his mind of the methods they would use to persuade him, and once they showed him what pleasures he might enjoy if he gave in to their desires. In spite of these threats and enticements, they did nothing to compel him, and in his heart, Lugh began to believe that they could not, that he must give willingly what they sought.

And when next the hole appeared in the hedge, and the owner of the white arm appeared with food and drink for him, he asked if this were true.

"It is true that they cannot take what you do not give, but in time you will be glad enough to do what they desire."

"Is that why you do their bidding?"

"Yes."

"But why do you not try to escape?"

"Why do you not try?"

"Because I am a prisoner behind this hedge of thorns."

At this there was silence for a time, but at length the voice spoke again. "There is no hedge; our bonds are of another kind."

"But if there is no hedge, then how is it that I can see and feel it; and how is it that all I can see of yourself is an arm and a hand?" But to this, the voice was silent.

Though in a while, Lugh heard the voice again, and this time it said, "The three have been talking together, and they have decided that if you do not choose one of them, today they will kill you."

"What can I do?" Lugh asked.

"Do you wish to escape?"

"There is nothing I would rather do."

"Then take my hand and believe that what I say is true!" Once again the slim white arm and hand appeared through the hedge.

Lugh took it, but still he hesitated.

"Hurry!" came the voice, "Why do you hesitate? The three are coming."

At which Lugh closed his eyes and in desperation pressed himself upon the hedge of thorns. But where he had thought to feel their harsh pricking, he felt nothing but air, and when he opened his eyes, he found that he stood upon a green mound amid a great circle of trees, and that his hand was clasping that of a slender girl whose black hair, red mouth, and bright eyes reminded him of a blackbird.

She pulled hard at his hand and urged him to hurry. "For the three are near, and once they discover that you have escaped, they will surely pursue us to the edge of the world."

Lugh looked behind him and saw only a featureless grayness on every side and nowhere that might be called an end to the sky or the land, if such indeed there were. "How may we escape?" he said.

"There are twelve gates to this place," said the girl, "and if you will but trust me, I will lead you through them all."

Lugh looked at her and knew that this was no trick, and when she offered him her hand again, he took it in his own without hesitation and followed where she led.

And that was the strangest journey that Lugh Strong Arm ever took, even in time to come when he undertook many deeds in the name of Arthur. He never forgot it, though if you were to ask him the how and the where of it, he would not tell you, only that there was much that seemed real and much unreal. Faces and voices and hands challenged them, but always the girl had answers for them where he would have had none, so that they came past each one until at last they stood in a different part of the wood where two great trees towered like sentinels. Here his guide stopped.

"This is the last gate of all," she said, "and through it I may not pass. But I will teach you the way so that you may depart."

"But surely, if I may pass, then so may you?"

But the girl shook her head. "I have been here too long. If I were to step beyond that gate I should at once crumble to dust."

And Lugh remembered stories he had heard of those who had returned from the Otherworld after what seemed only a few days but was in truth a hundred years. "Then how may I thank you?" he asked.

"I ask only that you remember me," said the girl. "Who knows? Perhaps I may find a way to escape. If not, I shall be here when you are dust."

Then she taught Lugh the secret words by which he might pass by the guardians of the last gate, and when he had spoken them, he found himself in a part of the great Wood that he knew. But of the entrance to that strange world in which he had been a prisoner, he could see nothing.

It is told that Lugh Strong Arm was changed from that time forth, and began to follow the course that brought him to become Arthur's greatest hero. But it is said also that of that time came the sealing of his fate, for when the three queens found that their prize was gone, they laid this *geas* upon him: that he should find love only with one woman, and that one, another's. But the gift of forgetting they withheld, so that even when Lugh became the lover of Gwenhwyfar the queen, he could not forget the slender girl whose black hair, red mouth, and bright eyes reminded him of a blackbird who had rescued him from prison. And this was the reason (though none knew it then), that when, long after, a barge drifted down to Camelot the Golden, bearing within it the body of a fair young girl with dark hair and white arms crossed upon her breast, that Lugh wept long and bitterly for what had been stolen from him, when he scarcely knew what it was that he had lost.

Of all the tales I found in the ancient scrolls, I believe this one speaks to me most deeply. Yet it fills me with fear when I read of the three queens, who are surely of the Otherworld and therefore evil. But it is for the nameless maiden who released the great warrior that my heart beats most strongly. In other tales I have heard, it is said that she was named Helaine and that she died for love of the hero Ancel. If the great bard is right, this may be a truer telling, one that speaks of a far more terrible fate—to be trapped in a place where the light of the Lord never shone.

LADY OF THE LAKE

The hawthorn flowers again
And the land is green,
But she lies all alone in her tower
Waiting the words to free her
Into the world she has lost.

So long divided, so long
Forced to follow the path of denial,
She had thought only death
could free her from this stony cell.

Now, as the year turns over,
As the hawthorn flowers again,
She hears the words of dreaming,
By one late come into her land.
Now, her chains unbound,
She feels her heart's blood
beating in the land,
and, with joyful singing,
sends her blessing forth upon the wind.

7
OWEIN OF THE RAVENS

o matter how old I become—and I have lived a good span of years—I will never cease to be astonished by the way things can happen right under one's nose while seeming no more than innocent pleasures. Games are such things, often hiding a far deeper truth than is at first apparent. Think of the game that Drustan and Issylt played on the ship that carried them from Ireland to Cornwall, a voyage that brought her to a loveless marriage and him to ever greater torment, for their love for each other lay behind the movement of each piece. ◆ Once a game was played that concerned the future of the Island of the Mighty—yet I suspect that none of those who looked on even suspected it at the time. The players were Arthur himself and his nephew Owein, and the stakes were as high as they could be—no less than the control of the war host of Britain. Now the story of this game is generally told only as the dream of one who lived long after the passing of the Ymerawdwr, but this deadly game was no dream, and I, who witnessed these events, will set down what truly happened.

As I read this tale, I cannot help but recall such visions as are recorded among our own kindred, such as Caedmon in the great abbey of Whitby, who found through a dream the ability to write poetry and song, though no man taught him how. These gifts were sent by God, it is true—but mayhap the vision of Rhonabwy came from some source, unknown to us now, equally deep and holy.

But there is a matter of even greater wonder about this tale. For it seems that the events of which the bard speaks took place long after the passing of the Lord Arthur, yet surely Taliesin himself was long dead by this time? A question pulls at my mind. Was he somehow preserved beyond the span of normal years, or was the bard able in some way to see beyond the days during which he lived? I push such thoughts away, lest I become too heretical.

There was a man called Iorweth ap Maredud, and he desired greatly to be overlord of Powys instead of his brother Madawg—however, this story does not concern him at all, and so we shall not hear of him again. It concerns rather one of his men, who was called Rhonabwy and a certain dream that he had while sleeping on the skin of a yellow ox in the house of Heilyn the Red, son of Cawgawn, son of Iddon, son of—well, never mind who he was the son of. Let us hear about Rhonabwy's dream.

This was the way of it: In his dream, Rhonabwy thought that he was riding towards the Ford of the Cross at Havren in the kingdom of Powys and that he saw coming towards him a figure that gave him cause to feel fear. The figure was a warrior dressed in green from the waist down, with a tunic of gold brocade sewn with green thread, and at his thigh a gold-hilted sword in a sheath of best cordovan leather. He wore a mantle of yellow brocade with patterns upon it sewn with green silk, and he rode a spirited, high-stepping horse that covered the ground so swiftly that he overtook Rhonabwy in two breaths. Such was the size of the warrior that Rhonabwy, even when mounted upon his horse, reached only to his thigh.

Rhonabwy gave the giant a polite greeting and asked to know who he was.

"Iddawg is my name, son of Mynyo. But I am better known by my nick-name, which is the Church of Britain."

"Why are you called that?" asked Rhonabwy.

"Because I was one of the messengers between Arthur and Medrawt before the Battle of Camlan, and every good word that Arthur spoke I made to sound like an insult. I did so because I was young and eager, and I desired very greatly that there should be battle between the two of them."

Now, even in his dream, Rhonabwy knew that the Battle of Camlan had taken place many hundreds of years before and that all these men in whose presence he stood had died there, including Arthur and Medrawt—though some still told a tale about Arthur being taken away by three royal women to a mysterious island somewhere in the West. Rhonabwy knew, of course, as all sensible people know, that such ideas were merely fables designed to entertain men of simple minds. Yet here he stood in the presence of a giant warrior who claimed he had been at Camlan, and he did not seem like a fable.

"Three days before the battle ended, I went to Scotland to do penance for my wicked deeds, but now I am returning to the camp of Arthur to join in the hosting of the Ravens. If you wish, you shall ride with me."

This invitation seemed to make even less sense to Rhonabwy, because if Arthur had been killed at Camlan along with all his warriors, how was it possible for Iddawg to be going to visit him?

While he was thinking this, another huge warrior upon a great black horse rode towards them. He was clad in red brocade sewn with yellow silk, and his mantle was fringed with gold. He swiftly overtook Rhonabwy and Iddawg and asked who this little fellow was that Iddawg had found. Though he did not much like being called a "little fellow," Rhonabwy had to admit the truth of it, and so he kept silent while the two warriors conversed.

Iddawg explained that he had found Rhonabwy upon the plain, and that he had invited him to ride to the hosting of the Ravens. Then the two fell to talking of who would be present, and Rhonabwy listened in astonishment to the names of heroes who were believed long dead in his time but who, it seemed, were coming together to fight a great battle against Osla Big Knife at a place called Caer Faddon. He heard much as well of one Owein, nephew of Arthur, whose warriors were called "Ravens" and from whom he might look for "entertainment" when he arrived at the camp.

And so the two huge warriors, with Rhonabwy riding between them (struggling to keep up, if the truth be told) crossed the plain of Argyngrog and came to the Ford of Rhyd y Groes on the Hafren, and there they found the tents of Arthur set up along the side of the road. And on a little flat islet in the center of the river, the pavilion of Arthur was set up. Arthur himself stood before it with a bishop upon his one side and a slender dark youth upon his other.

Rhonabwy stood in the presence of one already deemed fabulous and who, from his great size alone, could never be taken for a mortal. For Arthur was like a man of bronze, with his ruddy skin and red-gold hair and beard streaming down upon his breast. So powerful was he, indeed, that it seemed to Rhonabwy that he almost emitted a glow of light.

Iddawg and his companion (who was called Rhufawn) got down from their horses and splashed across the river to greet their lord. Rhonabwy hung back until Arthur saw him and demanded to know whence he came. When Iddawg explained, Arthur looked down at Rhonabwy and was silent. At length he sighed and said, "To think that men of his kind shall come to rule this land, after those who ruled it before them," which confused Rhonabwy deeply since it seemed impossible to him that he should be in the presence of so great and ancient a figure, who yet addressed him as a man of the future.

While this exchange had been taking place, a great commotion began along the river, and looking in that direction, Rhonabwy saw a second host of men approaching. They were dressed in black from head to foot, except for the fringes upon their mantles, which were of pure white, and they each had a tuft of ravens' feathers upon their helmets or about their persons, and the banner they bore was a raven upon a white ground.

IDDAWG AT THE FORD

Arthur stood up then and called, "Welcome, Owein, son of Urien; welcome to the Ravens."

And one of this host rode forward into the water upon his high-stepping black horse and called back, "Greetings to the war lord, Arthur; greetings, uncle."

Rhonabwy looked with keen interest to see this famed figure whose death song was still sung by bards in his own time. He saw a tall slender youth with shining black hair and eyes the color of cornflowers and a look of confidence about him that warned of a high mettled spirit. And he saw that although many of the warriors of Arthur greeted the Ravens of Owein, yet the latter chose to make camp on the farther bank of the river. But he was distracted from thinking such thoughts by Iddawg, who called him to come and watch the arming of Arthur. "For," said he, "the host must be at Caer Faddon by midday to meet with Osla Big Knife, and the Lord must first be armed for battle."

Then Rhonabwy saw a small hairy man with a great scarlet face come forward, and he had in his arms the sword of Arthur, which was named Caledflwch, having a design of two serpents upon the hilt. When the sword was drawn, it was as though fire came from the mouths of these creatures in two flames, and the light was such that no one might look at it. Then from a great pack, the small man drew forth a scarlet mantle with an apple of red gold at each corner and placed it about the shoulders of the Lord, and Rhonabwy remembered that it was said of this mantle, which was called Gwenn, that when it was wrapped about the body of the man who wore it, none might see where he walked, though he might see all that he wished.

And so the arming went on, with Arthur's shield, Prydwen, which had a magical likeness of God's Mother painted upon it, and Arthur's knife, Canwennan, that could cut the very air, and his mighty spear Rhongommiant, that no number of living men could turn aside, until at last the warrior stood ready, and the Great Dragon standard was unfurled at the head of its staff, and the whole host stood ready to depart.

At that moment, Owein came forward from the press of men gathered about their Lord and said loudly, "Uncle, will you play a game of gwyddbwyll with me?" and there was a sudden silence over all the throng.

Rhonabwy waited for Arthur to speak angrily to his nephew, but instead he merely smiled and said to the small man who carried his weapons, "Eiryn, fetch the board and the pieces." He called for two chairs and sat down and, when the gwyddbwyll board had been brought, Arthur and Owein began to play, while the rest of the host sat down to await the outcome of the game.

he game of which the Lord Arthur speaks is an old one, played in these islands long since. It is not unlike the game called chess, which was brought back with the brave knights who went forth to win back the Holy Land from the infidel.

When they were deeply into the game, a messenger hurried up to Arthur and said, "Lord, the Ravens are attacking your men and killing them with beak and claw!"

Arthur paused momentarily in his play and said, "Nephew, call off your Ravens!"

But Owein merely looked at the gwyddbwyll board and said, "Your move, Lord."

And so they continued to play, and all the time Rhonabwy, who did not quite dare to go and look, could hear the sound of a great commotion coming from the far side of the river.

Presently, when Arthur and Owein had finished one game of gwyddbwyll and had begun another, a second messenger rode up in a lather of sweat and cried out to Owein that Arthur's warriors had turned upon the Ravens and were inflicting terrible slaughter upon them.

Then it was Owein's turn to ask that Arthur call off his men, but Arthur merely said, "Play on, nephew."

And so they played, until a third warrior rode up, and he was dressed all in green and gold, with a helmet with a dragon's crest, the eyes of which blazed so furiously that no one dared look at them. And this messenger cried out that there was such terrible slaughter between Arthur's warriors and Owein's Ravens that soon there would be a scarcely a hale man among either host.

Then Arthur stood up and took four of the pieces in each of his great hands and crushed them to golden powder.

Owein looked at that work and, calling forward one of his retinue, told him to lower the standard of the Ravens.

At that there was peace between both sides, and Arthur and Owein cordially shook hands.

Rhonabwy, who had watched all this in some astonishment, shook his head over the strange actions of heroes (mythical or not) and turned to Iddawg for clarification. But the giant warrior only smiled and shrugged. And pointing to a ring that sparkled upon Arthur's finger, "See that," he said, "that is the ring of Arthur, and it has the property that will enable you to remember all that you have seen tonight."

At that moment a warrior came up to Arthur and said that Osla Big Knife had asked for a truce until a fortnight hence, and what should be his answer?

And Arthur said that he would grant the truce, so that both he and Owein might have time to reassemble their host and be ready for the battle. Then he mounted upon his great war steed from which he towered above all men there and in a great voice said, "Let all those who would take part in this battle with me meet upon the field of Caer Faddon in a fortnight in the morning. And those who shall not, need not." And he gave a great laugh and looked (Rhonabwy thought) straight at him.

Then the camp began to break up, and in the noise and bustle of that, Rhonabwy awoke; and whether he was a wiser man for the dream that he dreamed upon the yellow ox skin, or whether he was not, I cannot say, but I believe that he went away and spoke long and deeply to the two brothers who wished to be kings of Powys. Though whether they listened to him or not, I know not, for this is the end of the tale of Rhonabwy's dream and nothing else need concern us now.

TALIESIN AND RAVEN

Raven transforms me
In feathered black I dance
In cloak of dust I dance
In black wing-rags I dance

Raven had remade me
I see with his eyes
I feel with his senses
I gabble with his beak

Raven has taken me
I am shaken by his knowing
By a wisdom old as stone
By a strength pure as water

By his gift of perception
By his gift of laughter
By his gift of joy

8

DRUSTAN'S GHOST

I am Taliesin and I have walked where no mortal has ever walked. I have followed the secret ways between the worlds and entered the halls of Caer Siddi itself, where there is no time. ✒ Once when I visited that place, I met with one whom men now remember as Tristan, the Sad One, who loved the lady Issylt and lost his way amid the mazes of life because of it. To me he seemed no more than a ghost, an insubstantial rag of air that clung to a great stone carved with the ancient signs of ogham. But he told a story that seemed to me part of the pattern of the land, the deepest links between the Goddess and the mortal men who come to know her all too well. And so I tell it here, leaving those who would do so to interpret it as they wish. ✒ Once, I would have said, "This is true, or not true," but no longer do I look upon the ways of men and gods and try to untangle the meanings of what is said and done—most especially in the name of love. Now I tell simply what was told to me, plain and unvarnished, and leave others to decide for themselves what is meant. Perhaps the telling here will give rest to the shade of Drustan, who once walked this land as I do, and who came to know the hidden meanings of love as well as I know the trackways of the Great Wood.

ow sad is this tale! When I hear ill-fated Drustan speak of such passion as this, and of the terrible restlessness of spirit that comes in its wake, I give thanks to God that I am a monk and that such knowledge is forever closed to me. For what rest can two who love thus ever find?

I said that I would follow her forever, and so I have. But now she is gone where I may not be (unless she comes for me), and all I can do is sing of our joy and our sorrow, of the love that burned us and left the land riven and unhealed.

All because of a cup, drunk without thought in a midsummer gale on the ocean with the salt spray blowing in our faces and the gulls flying high above the swaying masthead. So much to tell, and so little time in which to tell it, before the sun rises again, and I am bound once more to the stone.

It was winter when my father, Marcus Flavius Cunomorus, self-styled king of Dumnonia, first showed signs of the sickness that was to change the lives of us all. He had been out hunting, as was his usual practice, but this time he came home a changed man. Before he was familiar—bluff, hearty, a big man in every sense. After, he was meaner, pinched, somehow fearful as well as angry, as though at an adversary neither he nor any of us could see.

He sent for me that same afternoon, and when I arrived in his private chamber, I found Andret there also. There was no love lost between my brother and me, but we both knew when our father's wishes were not to be refused.

He looked at us both in turn with eyes that had grown feral and red rimmed in the space of a few hours. Then he smiled, which was, in its way, as terrible. He took something from a pouch at his belt and laid it on the table before us. It looked like a long, pale-gold hair, finer than the finest harp string I ever possessed.

"There," said my father, smiling that happy, empty smile. "There is her token. You must do the rest."

Andret, who was always the bolder of us when the need arose, took the chance. "What is it you wish us to do, father?" he asked.

Our father's smile vanished. "What!" he cried, "can it be that you are too stupid to understand? What must I do to explain it to you?" He paced slowly around the table, towering over us, though we were neither of us beardless boys. "I see that I must spell out even the most obvious things," he said at last, but the way he said it brought a chill to my heart. "Very well, then. This hair is from the head of the woman I shall marry. You must find her and bring her to me. Is that clear enough for my two brave young sons?"

That was obviously as clear as anything our father was ever going to say to us. So we looked at each other, and when Andret shrugged, I picked up the golden hair, intending to cut it in twain, one-half for Andret, one for me. At once, a strange feeling overcame me. Everything looked suddenly altered, as though it was not quite solid any more. Both my father and my brother were changed as well, at least my father was more or less as he had become in those last few hours, while Andret became suddenly "dangerous"—leaner, harder, more ratlike. All the small, unhappy tricks he had played on me were suddenly brought to mind. In that moment, I hated Andret with an all-consuming hatred; I found that, without thinking, my hand had sought the hilt of my dagger.

Then, as quickly as it had come, the mood passed, to be replaced by an even stronger feeling—a desire to discover the owner of the hair. It was so deep and strong a feeling that I was halfway to the door before Andret knocked me down. We began struggling with a silent ferocity quite foreign to our usual battles and might indeed have done each other serious hurt had not our father fallen upon us roaring and dragging us bodily apart. He tore the golden hair from my hand, cut it in two with a swift slash of his knife, and gave one piece to each of us.

"Go!" he said, with scarcely contained anger. "Get out of my sight, and don't come back until you have found her!"

Andret and I backed off, glaring at each other, but strangely, the moment that he had a piece of the hair, my desire to attack him vanished, as apparently did his to get at me. We left the chamber together, hastened to our rooms and gathered a few necessary possessions, took our horses, and left the court.

We went separate ways, myself going west, Andret north. I never saw my brother again, nor do I know what happened to him. Perhaps he wandered into a land where her influence did not stretch, and there found rest. Perhaps he fell victim to outlaws or other evil powers. In the end, I think, he was lucky.

For myself, I pressed on through lands that were at first familiar but soon became less so and were finally strange. I had no clear idea where I was going, but there is little doubt that I was in some way guided by my possession of the golden hair.

After a while I entered the forest, a region of that vast, dark wood of which the bards have sung and which is called in the tongue of the French, *Broceliande*. It was a place not much visited in those times, and its vast enclaves were little explored. It was not a place I would have chosen to go, but I had no choice, so completely was I bound by the power of the golden hair.

And so I came, after a period of traveling that has no borders in my mind, to the place where I was always meant to be.

At sunset I came to an edge of the Wood and looked out upon the sea. It stretched flat and empty to the horizon, where I could just discern the shape of hills. Beached and waiting on the verge of the land was a small coracle of the kind much favored along the shores of Dumnonia. I knew well how to sail it, and since this was the way I must go, I stepped aboard. Taking the small, single paddle, I pushed off from the shore of Britain and set sail for the other shore, a land that was no land, where men never ventured.

And though it had seemed far off when I first glimpsed it from the edge of the forest, now it seemed that distance was deceptive, for it took me less than a day of paddling to reach that other shore. It seemed to me that the coracle knew its own way and needed little effort on my part to steer it. This did not surprise me, and at last I did little but lay back in the shallow craft and take out my part of the golden hair and look at it.

If it had seemed fair and bright before, now it seemed to glow, and by this I knew that I was nearing my destination. Sure enough, when next I raised my eyes from the contemplation of my token, I found that the shore was near. Great, frowning cliffs rose from the sea close at hand. There I saw a channel leading into a bay, and my fine craft was easy to steer between the rocks until it lay at rest on a margin of white sand.

I stepped ashore, and for the first time since I had laid hand upon the hair, I felt at peace. There and then I sat down upon a rock and took out my harp, which had suffered surprisingly little from its journey and was quickly tuned. I began to play, softly at first, an ancient tune I had learned from a traveling bard only the winter before. So lost did I become in the music that I neither heard nor saw her approach. Only when I had played enough did I look up and see her.

From that moment, my fate was sealed.

The hair that had come from her head in no wise matched the splendor of its companions. Like white gold it fell, to her hips and beyond, and it framed a face more beautiful to me than the dawn. I loved her at once, with a deep and unshakeable love. In a thousand years it has not dimmed.

Her voice, when she spoke to me, was as sweet as the sweetest songbird's and matched everything about her that was itself matchless. "Welcome, Drustan. That was sweetly played."

To hear praise from her lips was to dwell in Tir na nOg itself, and I knew myself utterly lost from that moment. When she stretched forth her hand, I placed mine willingly within it and went with her into the silence of that place.

ere is one of the great mysteries of love, sacred and profane. I take the words "to dwell in Tir na nOg" to mean to dwell, as it were, in paradise. That goal, at least, is known to those who, like myself, follow the way of Christ. Yet, how different are the means by which that state is sought!

Caer Siddi, of which the bard makes mention, seems to me an outlying island of that same otherworldly place of which the Lord Taliesin speaks so often in these pages. Certainly, it is a place where time, such as binds mortal men, is all but unknown. Perhaps, therefore, we may see in it another aspect of that blessed state sought by both monks and lovers!

And so I dwelt there, on the island of Caer Siddi, which has also been called Spiral Castle, with the woman I came to know as Issylt, though I know now that she has many other names. And time passed not at all it seemed, though the sun rose and set and rose again. By its light we walked on the sweet grass of the island or climbed the hills until we could look out at the restless sea; or else we lay at rest beneath the shade of the apple trees that grew in the sheltered groves amid the valleys of that place. And at night I sang to her and played such music as I had never known was in me, and I loved her as deeply as a man can love a woman and with all the fierceness of a consuming flame.

In those flames I was myself, somehow, consumed. And when I had no more will or wish to be anything other than I was, or to know any other life, Issylt came to me and told me that we must depart. When I sought to protest, though weakly, she laid a finger on my lips and said, smiling,

"It must be so, my love. It must be so."

Then, though I had seen no other living soul save animal or bird in that land since first I set foot upon it, suddenly there were people who came forward with rich clothing for us both and who washed us in scented water and garbed us as a king and queen. Then they led us to the shore where a great ship awaited, and we went aboard.

Two things I remember from that voyage, which somehow took longer than my own short passage from shore to shore. One was the game we played on the first day, a strange game played with jeweled pieces on a golden board, and the second is the cup with which we pledged each other as we sat together on the deck of the ship, with its great sail billowing above us, and the salt spray on our faces, and gulls flying high above the swaying masthead.

This must be the very game to which the great bard refers in the story he called "Owein of the Ravens."

A simple cup it was, though of gold, as was everything that came of Spiral Castle. But the drink. Ah! That was not simple. In it lay the fate of the land, though I knew it not, and in it also lay the bitter draught that was to bind me here until the ending of all things.

Issylt, when she offered it to me, said only, "Let us pledge ourselves each to other and swear that we will abide by what must be."

I drank, and with that draught came both joy and endless sorrow—joy because it sealed our love across all time; sorrow because it brought also knowledge. For I knew then what had changed my father. I seemed to see in my mind his meeting with Issylt that day of hunting, and the pledge made between them for the good of the land. For she was not made for any one man or for any mortal lover. Her destiny was greater. So, too, was my father's, for despite his Roman pretensions, his blood was far older and carried the strength of the land. By their mating would come a new flowering, the dried-up wells would flow again despite the harm done long ages since by Amangons and his men.

By this, I understand Taliesin to refer to the terrible story of the ancient king Amangons, who desired the love of one of those women who had dedicated her life to guarding one of the sacred wells of Britain. When he forced her to lie with him against her will, the well that she guarded dried up, and from this, others followed suit, until the land was barren. Later, in the time of Arthur, that evil was undone, as is here suggested, by the marriage of Issylt and King Marcus. Though these matters are strange to me, from a deeper reading of these tales, I believe that kings in those days more often married the land than any mortal woman, Jesu protect us!

For the rest, the story is well known: How the Sad One "Tristan" brought "Iseult" to King Mark, and how he used her ill so that she began to love the son who had brought her to Dumnonia rather than the father she was meant to wed. And how she and the son became lovers and fled to the forest to dwell there in lawless bliss. So, too, is it told that the land grew sick, and the wells remained dry and the fields fallow, until there was war between King Mark and the emperor Arthur and great evil besides. And it is said that Tristan fell sick at last and died, and that she who loved him perished from sorrow and was laid by his side, and that two thorn trees grew from their grave and put forth red and white flowers that twined together.

Such is the story, but it happened otherwise. The truth is that our love was too strong for the tide of fate that bore us. The mating of my father's blood with the blood of the Goddess was not to be, and the land grew sick because of it. But what is not told is how that evil was undone and what truly became of Tristan and Iseult.

We fled, it is true, from the madness of my father to the safety of the Wood. But there time does not cease to move as it had for us on the island, for once departed from Caer Siddi, no mortal may return again. And with that knowledge came a bitter sorrow that I could not transcend. It threatened even our love, though that grew no cooler, and became like a sword laid between us.

At length, Issylt spoke to me of the land and of its sickness, from which we were saved within the enclave of the Wood. And when she had spoken, we were silent for a long while, until I found the words to say what had begun to fill my mind of late—that I could not bear to grow old while she remained unchanged; that I would sooner die than watch our love grow cold.

Thus it was that Issylt spoke of a way in which we might always be one, until time itself ceased and the lives of the Wood were rolled up and laid away until the next day of creation.

Easy enough, it seemed to me then, to sleep the long sleep and yet be free, to be bound forever to my love. But now I know that the ways of the people of Caer Siddi are not for mortals, any more than our ways are for them. But knowing nothing of the fate I was sealing, I drank again of the cup, the second draught that brings sleep and forgetting. But I did not forget, and my sleep is shallow. You who walk here, who see me and hear my words, understand this better than I ever shall.

Yet I believe that one day she will come. Time means nothing in Caer Siddi. It is but a moment since I drank, though by the reckoning of men, a thousand years mayhap have passed, and from that moment I have waited. The land has flowered again, and sickened and flowered many times since then. But still I wait, and soon, I believe, she will come—and we shall both be set free.

DRUSTAN AND ISSYLT

Through her brow and downward,
following the body's curve,
the lightning of love
strikes at the heart of the Grail.

The trembling of his brows
is all to say:
It is done, the time of dreams—
now we are one. . .

And from her hand
the speckled bird flies free.

MELWAS' HALL

9

THE ABDUCTION AND RESCUE OF GWENHWYFAR THE QUEEN

wenhwyfar—sometimes called Guinevere—was well named the "White Shadow," but I had another name for her, the "White Weaver," for assuredly she wove her webs around all our hearts. Lugh, especially, was her slave from the moment their eyes met, but the rest of us also: Arthur, Gawain, Geraint—every one of them saw something within her that made her not only Arthur's queen but also Corn Mother, Goddess of the Land, holder of Sovereignty's gift. ❧ How to explain these things to you who may read this so far in the future? For yes, in one sense Guinevere was never a woman of mortal flesh or spirit, and the truth about her can be told in so many different ways. I might say that she came from the Faery How of Cameliarde and that her father Leodgrance was, like Merlin, of otherworldly stock, but what would that mean to you? Better if I say she was queen, that she came of an ancient bloodline of the land, and that

she knew the old ways of worship and wisdom as surely as Merlin, or Morgain, or I.

I have even heard it muttered—usually behind a hand—that Gwenhwyfar was the daughter of a giant and that Arthur won her only after terrible slaughter and on the death of her father. As to that, there is no truth in it, but I have also heard another story: that once while he rode hunting, the King met a lady in the deep wood. He bedded her on the grassy floor and brought her with him back to his stronghold at Camulodunum and made her his wife.

But the truth of the matter is that when Arthur married Gwenhwyfar, he married the land, for she was the outward sign of the Sovereignty and brought with her the gift of the apple tree that never dies and always bears fruit. But in all the times I was in her presence, I never felt that I knew her, nor indeed that I came within leagues of understanding what drove her.

But the tale I would tell now concerns another time, when Arthur was older—though years seemed not to have marked his queen—and when the land was for the most part at peace. Then there came to Camulodunum a hero named Melwas, who named himself King of the Summer Country (though all who heard him speak thus made the sign of the horns against ill luck). But he seemed no more than a man for all that, and it is said that the women he bedded found no fault with him in that way. And so he came to be accepted among the war band, and men soon forgot that he had claimed a title beyond their understanding and took him for one no different from themselves.

But all the while, he cast looks of longing and desire towards the Lady Gwenhwyfar, and when she would not return them, he grew bold and maddened. So that when one day it was found that the queen was missing, though none knew how she had been spirited away, and after that it was found that Melwas was also gone, it did not take long to surmise who the two riders had been, seen before daylight leaving Camulodunum, strangely muffled in cloak and hood and heading west towards the Summer Country.

At once Arthur mustered the war band and set forth in pursuit, though many muttered that such a course could lead to no good and that the way ahead must soon leave this world behind. Only Gwalchmai and Lugh (who were said to love the Lady Gwenhwyfar equally) refrained from questioning their lord, and because of this Cei and Bedwyr, Cador and Ydol also kept silence and hastened to keep pace with their grim lord, who drove his mount hard from the anger that raged within him.

For a while the way was easy and the trail not hard to follow, but in a while the character of the land changed. There were less places that men knew from hunting there, and soon these were gone also. The war band rode through a dim world that seemed scarcely there at all, at which many were seen to cast looks of apprehension over their right shoulders, while others kept their faces between their horses' ears and looked neither right nor left.

After they had followed that road for no longer than it would take to cover eight leagues from Camulodunum, they were in a place unfamiliar to any one among them. Where there should have been trees on either hand, there were fields of standing corn, and though it seemed past the midpoint of the day, the sun stood still in the sky and burned down upon the warriors until they began to tire and their mounts to stumble beneath them.

At last Arthur called a halt and, looking at them grimly, said that he required none to follow him that were afraid of that place, but that he would go forward alone if need be, while they waited for his return. There were those who felt mindful to remain there, but when they fell to thinking of how it would be to be lost in that place without their leader, they all pressed to be allowed to go where Arthur went. Without a word, he lead the way onward, seeming to know where he should go.

Sure enough, before long, there was the gleam of sunlight on water, and the war band came to a place of creeks and narrow waterways surrounded by great reed beds that seemed alive with birds of many kinds. There, in the center of that strange, shifting landscape, was a hall of wood, ornately carved, with a ring of sharpened stakes set round it and a gate firmly barred. Arthur rode up to it, with

Lugh and Gwalchmai, Bedwyr and Cei at his back, and set up a cry that made all the birds on the margins of the waterways rise into the air on sudden wings. The cry was to Melwas to come forth.

Soon enough the head of the Lord of the Summer Country appeared above the row of sharp spikes, looked down upon the warriors of Arthur, and laughed aloud to see them there.

"Melwas, you have my wife," said Arthur with iron in his voice. "Give her up or pay the price with your life."

"I think not, Arthur," Melwas answered. "You have no power here unless I give you leave; only thus have you come so far," and he raised a hand and spoke words of command at which one-half of the war band found themselves unable to move either hand or foot. Then all knew for certain (if any still doubted it) that Melwas was no ordinary man.

But Arthur did not cease from looking at Melwas, eye to eye, and he said, "This quarrel is between you and I, Melwas of the Summer Country. Come forth and we will settle it man to man."

At this Melwas only laughed and said, "Since I am not a man, that would be no contest. But if you, or one among you, will offer to meet my champion, then it shall be decided thus which one of us will keep your queen."

Lugh and Gwalchmai would both have spoken then, but Arthur held up his hand and said, "I alone shall answer this challenge," and he got down from his gray steed and drew the sword Caledfwlch that men say was given to him by the Goddess of the Lake and set himself ready to meet whatever might come.

Presently the gate of Melwas' stronghold opened, and there came forth a fierce and terrible warrior, a span taller than any there. He was tattooed all over with spiraling patterns and carried a great axe in his hands. Many there were who deemed him kin to the Great Gome with whom Gwalchmai had played the Beheading Game and won, and even Lugh of the Strong Arm drew back a pace when he saw the size of the warrior. But Arthur merely smiled and said, "This one has need of cutting down to size," and he went forward unafraid.

Of that combat men tell many tales that are even longer in the telling than this whole adventure; therefore, I will say only that it lasted throughout the long hours of the afternoon, and at the end of it, the grass was stained red with blood, and the breaths of the two warriors came harsh and heavy. But neither might find advantage over the other, for while Melwas' champion had the strength of ten men and the swiftness of the Otherworld about his movements, Arthur was guarded by the power of his sword.

And at last Melwas himself appeared in the gateway and bade them stop. Then he summoned his followers within to bring forth the Lady Gwenhwyfar and said that she might settle this dispute between them, for no other way was there that the matter could end, unless it be in bloody battle or dark enchantment.

Then Gwenhwyfar, whom none might look upon without loving her for the beauty and gentleness of her appearance, took thought on how best to mend this sorry matter. And at the end she spoke thus (and let it be known that those who say these words were spoken of the woman Issylt and her lover Drustan are liars): "Let this be the judgment between Arthur and Melwas: that I shall be with one while the leaves are upon the trees and with the other while they are not, and to this both must agree."

Then Arthur and Melwas looked long at each other and at Gwenhwyfar, and so it was agreed between them both. Melwas spoke first and said that he would have her while there were no leaves on the trees (for he deemed that then the nights would be longest). And Arthur laughed and said, "Holly and ivy and yew keep their leaves until death. You have lost, Melwas; my queen is restored to me."

And for that his given word was binding, Melwas gave up the Lady Gwenhwyfar, though he did so with ill grace. The war band found that movement was restored to them, and so they left that place and returned to Camulodunum, which seemed but a short ride after all from the Summer Country. But it is said that, afterwards, Lugh of the Strong Arm returned there and slew Melwas, but there are many tales told of Arthur's greatest warrior, and this is not the place to say which are true and which are not.

I sense that here the great bard is concealing something that he may have made plain elsewhere, perhaps in the ancient book wherein he chronicled the mysteries of the Lord Arthur. Sometimes it seems to me that these are not real people of whom he writes, but insubstantial ghosts who belong only to the realm of story and have no place under God's holy sky. Yet I must confess that in my inmost heart, I yearn to have had a single glimpse of the woman so many were willing to die for—whether mortal or faery, she must have been possessed of a beauty only a little less than that of the angels.

SEASONS OF THE LAND

1: KING IN SHADOW

Spilled out
the seed rots in the ridged furrow.
Hunting ended,
a horn calls out in the dead land.
Word travels swiftly on the dry roads:
"The king in Shadow!
The sword rusts in its sheath of stone!"

2: THE QUEEN MAD

Cracks in the Round Table—
her father's wedding gift.
Prospect of a shining circle—
and through the dull ache of loss:
the shadowed kingdom
the empty land. Broken
the things that once were;
love lost in the turn of a year.

3: THE YOUNG HUNTSMAN

The sun's beams
bright on his shield of silver;
earth warmed by his coming;
dry land filled with the heat of spring.
In his hands the sword flames—
seeds sprout in the beds of the land.
Scattering life, the huntsman comes—Gawain,
Galahad, Graal—and the murmur:

"The Queen's come back"
makes summer's kingdom
burn again, turning toward evening
and the birth of a bright star.

Part III
LATER TALES

10

GRISANDOLE

Not many think of Merlin as having a sense of humor. After all, when you are the Guardian of the Sacred Land, the Servant of the Lake, and the advisor to the greatest king ever to rule over Logres, there isn't much to laugh about. But once, on a dark day when all the world seemed over, I heard Merlin tell a story about his own youth. He told it straight-faced, mind you; not by so much as the blink of an eye or a quiver of the lips did he betray the humor of the situations he described. Some will say the events he related never happened, that no such emperor ever existed, and no such story is told of the empress. But who are we to question the Old One, who lived from the beginning and is still living now, for all I know? This is what I heard him say:

ell me this if you can: Why should a woman want to be a man? Avenable did, though she was of noble blood and wanted for nothing. True, her father had been banished for some trifling offence, and her circumstances were somewhat reduced, but she could still have lived out her life in a perfectly ordinary way: married, borne children, grown

fat, and eventually died, surrounded by a mourning husband, sons, and daughters. Instead, she wanted to be a man, "to live in a man's world and experience all that men experience." I can't see why she should have wanted that, since most men are such fools and seem to spend most of their lives hacking each other about with swords or trying to knock each other off their horses. As though it were fun to keep kissing the ground!

Still, Avenable was determined, and eventually her determination led her to run away and, having disguised herself as a youth, to take service in the guard of no lesser person than the emperor of Rome.

This is where the story becomes interesting, because at the time, the emperor was having a series of nightmares—or rather, the same nightmare over and over again, in which he saw a huge, rapacious sow being chased through the city by twelve boars. Of course, being an emperor, he took this dream to be an omen of some kind, but could find no one brave enough to tell him whether it was for good or ill.

I knew what the dream meant, but I was not about to walk into the emperor's court and tell him. However, there was an injustice to be set right, and there was Avenable—or rather Grisandole as "he" now called himself. So I quickly devised a plan to enable me to explain the dream, put right the injustice, and show Grisandole the error of her ways.

The first anyone else knew of this scheme was a few weeks later when the emperor, his wife, and their household—including of course, Grisandole—were staying for a few days in one of the imperial country villas. There, just as the whole family was about to dine, a huge stag with vast branching antlers and one white foot burst into the hall and stood panting before the astonished gathering. It is said—and I will vouch for it because, of course, I was the stag (a mere matter of the transformative will)—that the beast spoke, telling the emperor that it knew of his dreams and that only one person could tell him what they meant: the Old Wise Man who lived in the depths of the forest near his palace. After which, the beast vanished.

Of course, the Old Wise Man was me again, but no one would have believed me, let alone permitted me to get near the emperor, if I had simply wandered into the court asking to see him. While I might, indeed, have used some other method, suitably spectacular, to gain admittance, doing so would not have solved the problem of Grisandole.

Well, in typically extravagant fashion, the emperor offered a huge reward to anyone who could find the Old Wise Man and bring him to the court for questioning. Everyone, including Grisandole, set off in search of the prophet, and everyone was unsuccessful. I am not to be found unless I want to be—which I did, in this instance, but not by just anyone. I waited until most of the seekers had given up—though I kept on encouraging Grisandole, showing the occasional tip of an antler in the forest, or maybe the merest glimpse of an old ragged man. Then I went to a clearing where I knew she was resting, and putting on the guise of the stag with one white foot again, I told her what she must do to find and capture the Old Wise Man.

Very obedient was Grisandole, a sensible girl for all her strange fancies. She got five of her young companions-in-arms to come with her into the forest and set up a table with a white linen cloth over it and plenty of food. They lit a fire and sat down to wait. Sure enough "the Old Wise Man" soon appeared, tucked into the meal, and then went to sleep, snoring like a pig in front of the fire. It was an easy task for the six of them to bind me. In the morning, we all set off for to the emperor's palace.

On the way, three small events occurred, which I mention here only as an example of the way I like to work sometimes. Mystification is not always enough, and being able to change one's shape or conjure things from the air isn't either.

The first incident took place when we camped for the night in a field. Grisandole lay down with the other young men, putting me in the middle. I couldn't help laughing when I thought that not one of them knew she was a girl, and I suppose my laughter got the better of me, because in the end, one of the companions came over and told me in no uncertain terms to keep quiet, waving a sword under my nose to make certain I understood.

The second incident took place when we happened to pass a crowd of mendicants waiting for alms outside an abbey. They were a thin, unwashed, malodorous bunch, and when I saw them—or rather when the Old Wise Man saw them—he began laughing so hugely that he almost fell off the horse to which he was tied. Grisandole and the rest looked at each other with looks that said, "Poor fellow; mad as a cuckoo."

But when the next incident occurred, they seemed more concerned. This event took place when we all stopped to hear Mass in a church along the way, as some of the six wanted to give thanks for the reward they were going to get for finding me. While we were in the church, we saw a young squire leave his place three times, strike his astonished master a blow in the face, and then stand there looking dazed, claiming that an unknown agency had made him do it.

No, it was not me who caused this last event to happen, but I did start laughing again, so loudly that Grisandole took me outside, took out her sword, and demanded to know what I was about. I didn't tell her, but I did call her a sly, deceitful villain, which not only made her angry, but also worried her, in case I might somehow have penetrated her disguise. However, I refused to say another word, and in fact uttered not another sound until we reached the emperor's palace, where I was led before him, still bound, and commanded to explicate the dream.

The exchange that followed went like this:

Emperor: Are you the Old Wise Man?

Me: URRGGHH!

Emperor: I see. And do you know the meaning of the dream I have had every night for a month?

Me: URRGGHH!

Emperor: He is clearly mad. Take him away.

Me: I am most certainly not mad, sir. But I will only speak before all your nobles and your empress and everyone of the court.

Emperor: (looking surprised): Very well. We shall call our vassals before us
  on the morrow.

So I was taken away, given a bath—which, truth to tell, I was glad of, since playing flea-ridden old men is hard work even for me—then fed and given a clean and comfortable bed to sleep in. Of course, an armed guard was placed on the door, just to remind me not to try and go anywhere.

Next morning, we all appeared before the emperor in great splendor, including Grisandole with her armor polished so that you could see your face in it, and her sword so sharp it could have cut the wind. They brought me in, and as soon as I saw the empress, I started laughing again, falling on the ground and rolling about, biting my beard like a madman. Which is what everyone thought I was, until I suddenly stopped, stood up and addressed the emperor in my normal voice.

"Sir, I will explain everything to you. Those who brought me here will have told you of my laughter on other occasions. No doubt they thought me crazed. But each time there was a reason for my merriment. When we saw many men and women begging for bread and water, I laughed because all the time there was a treasure buried beneath their feet. Later, we saw a squire who struck his master three times, and again I knew that beneath his feet lay a fortune. Each blow that he struck was but a token of the evils of riches which cried out to him from the very earth. Now I laugh because of the meaning of your dream, which signifies this . . . ."

I paused, I must admit, for effect, waiting until I knew that I had everyone's attention. Then I proceeded to tell the emperor that his empress had twelve ladies-in-waiting who were, in fact, young men in disguise, and that they had certainly been doing more than merely waiting on her for the past six months. This was the meaning of the rapacious sow and the twelve boars that chased it through the city.

Uproar! Screams! Cries for mercy, death, clemency, execution! The empress and her "ladies" were held, examined, and the truth found to be as I had described it. Then, while everyone was still gasping for breath, I told the emperor about the other occasion when I had laughed: when I had looked at Grisandole sleeping between her sword-brothers and known that she was really a girl.

More uproar and outrage! But, of course, this time there was no real crime intended, and Grisandole had served the emperor well. Apart from which, when he had a good look at her, the emperor decided that Avenable, as we may call her again, was really rather beautiful, and that once the empress had been executed for her crimes, he would need a new consort. As I said, Avenable was very well connected.

I vanished, of course, leaving the usual cryptic message in letters of fire on the wall to be interpreted later by a passing Latinist to the effect that Merlin was both the stag and the Old Wise Man.

As for the rest, Avenable's father was pardoned and his lands restored, while his daughter became the new empress. As far as I know they lived happily enough. But I still cannot fathom why Avenable wanted to be a man, nor for that matter why she never seems to have forgiven me for setting her life in order.

T here is a mystery here which I find quite fascinating. In none of the many tales that are told of the terrible enchanter Merlin—whom many say was the devil's son—have I heard that he visited Rome. Yet here he speaks quite naturally of it, as though it were a fact. Not even in the great bard's book is such a journey mentioned, which leads me to wonder if there are not many other such tales lost forever in the darker chambers of history.

SNOW WIVES

Snow came over the hill's shoulder,
cold as moonlight,
bright as spear blades on the fell.
And the snow men walked
cheek by jowl
with warriors of steel,
until, in the morning, sunlight
stole shadows from the trees,
dreams from dreamers,
blood from stones.

And the snow came still
under star and moon
to lay its patterns on the earth,
to kiss all stones with a breath of ice,
to dance in the eyes
of the women of snow.
Snow came seeking them,
snow shadowed them,
snow dogged their feet—
peering into eyes and mouths
loading heads with ice.

But no snow maidens
danced to meet them;
no snow wives came
to warm their night.

Instead, snow came
over the hills' hard edges
lonely as crippled streams.

Swept away,
night fell back into silence
and shutters closed
on lightless windows in the night.

11

THOMAS AND THE BOOK

I have written of the secret long kept in the abbey of Ynys Witrin—the ancient book written, perhaps, by the bard Taliesin himself and known only to the abbots of the place—and of my own involvement in guarding this secret. I have spoken also of the parchment pages Abbot Thomas handed me, which told the tale of another monk named Thomas who lived at Ynys Witrin. Though to this day I do not know if the Thomas of the tale is my Abbot Thomas or another, it is clear that my Thomas believed it to be part of the heritage of ancient wisdom referred to in the tale as the Voice of Tradition. ❧ I have searched the shelves of the library here in the abbey, and I believe that I have discovered the text of which this story tells. It is called Perlesvaus, and the belief is that it was written here at the abbey, but at a time when it seems neither the great bard nor the Abbot Thomas I knew could have penned it. There is much that remains mysterious in all of this, yet I have no doubt that this tale should be gathered with the others, and that I am right to include the vision of this Thomas among those of the great bard and his successors.

In the midst of darkness, as the weight of the night lay upon him with all its depths and mystery, Thomas became aware of light, dim at first, but growing to such strength that he was almost unable to bear it. He sat up with a stifled cry, shading his eyes against the fierce burning in the night. And lo, the light spoke, with each word turning and flickering as though to a harmony of sound and light.

"Thomas, know you who it is who speaks to you?"

"I know not."

"I am the master of masters, the one from whom it was said, all wisdom cometh."

"Voice, I am filled with doubt."

The Voice was silent, flickering strongly. Then it spoke again. "I am come to set aside your doubts. I am come to teach you a great mystery that you may set it down in writing for others that come after. I am the Voice of Tradition."

Thomas was silent in his turn, having nothing that he might say to express the wonder he felt. "Indeed," he thought, "I do dream most deeply this night."

But the Voice seemed to hear even his thoughts, for it said, "You do not dream. Here is a book that shall tell you how the line of which you come is part of the shape of time and follows that shape truly."

Thomas then found that he was holding a small book in his hands, and that the light had gone as utterly as if it had never been, and that he was awake indeed in his small stone cell with the hard cot beneath him. A great feeling of misery overcame him, as well as a deep curiosity, so that he rose, found a lamp and struck a light, and looked at what he held.

To many it would have seemed strange, a wonder in itself, for there were few enough such things in that time. But to Thomas it was a book, and like all books, it consisted of many sheets of vellum bound in leather, clasped about with bands of metal. It was not an especially rich seeming book; Thomas had seen richer. Its binding was plain, and the clasps that fastened it were neither of silver or gold. Like lead they seemed, dull and heavy.

Slowly and with the care of one used to handling precious objects, Thomas opened the clasps and turned back the cover. A faint scent, as of incense, rose from the pages, which seemed new and unread. He opened the first folio and stared at the letters without at first understanding them. All of his attention went to the initial letter, which was written after an earlier style that he himself used. He remembered its like from other books in the scriptorium of his monastery and was, for a moment, back there with Brother Blaise at his elbow, hearing the harsh old voice, critical as ever, finding fault with his efforts to form the letters in the years before his efforts met with silence, the greatest praise the old master could offer.

Thomas brought his mind back to the book in his hands and to the picture within the balanced uprights of the first letter. Like a window into another world, it showed a forest scene with a clearing in which there was a fountain. Every detail of the ornate carving around the fountain's base was pictured so clearly that Thomas could read every mark; and where the water fell in a silvered rain from the fountain, he could almost hear the splash of the drops in the marble coping. With an effort, Thomas brought his attention to bear on the words. He read:

> Here is the Book of thy Lineage.
> Here begin the Terrors.
> Here begin the Marvels.

He read no further but closed the book with a sharp snap that echoed in the confined space of his cell. A terrible panic seized him. He trembled through his whole body, and such a dread was upon him that for a long time he could neither move nor speak. Then at last he said, into the darkness beyond the flickering rush light, "Do I indeed dream?"

No voice came back from the corners of the room, but Thomas needed none, for he knew that he was awake. Then a weariness fell upon him that was as heavy as had been the fear of moments before, and without thought, he put out the light and lay down, placing the little book underneath his head, from where he drew in a fading breath of incense with his last waking thought.

Habit awoke him, and he was halfway to his knees with the first words of prayer upon his lips before he remembered the events of the night. He forced himself to remain awhile with eyes closed until he had completed *Ave* and *Paternoster*, only then opening his lids a crack and turning his head towards the bed.

He had been so certain that the book would be gone, that when it was truly no longer there, it took him several moments to realize it. The shock brought him fully to his senses, and he stared at the place where he had slept, recalling again the details of the night and the words of the Voice. Had he, then, dreamed in truth? Bending closer to the bed he saw that, impressed faintly into the thin mattress, was a shape—not the shape of his own head, but a small, square indentation. Again it was a moment before he understood: The book had been real; his dream true. But (the thoughts coming faster now), if so, then where? And how? And better still, why? Thomas sank back upon his heels and closed his eyes. Like a dim echo of the fiercely burning light he had seen, he saw a shining there, and like a faint, scarce heard echo of the Voice, he heard words that told him what he must do, and how, and when. But still, they did not tell him why.

Next morning, Thomas rose early and, with an assurance born of inward certainty, set forth on the road. He went west, walking, taking nothing with him except enough food and water for a day's traveling. Long before that day was over, he reached a meeting place of four ways. There was a Cross there. At its foot knelt a strange beast like no other that had been seen. It had the head of a sheep, whiter than snow, and its feet were those of a dog. Between these two points, there was the body of a wolf that yet had the tail of a lion. It was able to go upright upon its hind legs like a man, as Thomas discovered when it rose up before him. Thomas looked at the beast and the beast looked at him, and then it turned itself about and set off leading, and Thomas followed.

All through that afternoon the beast kept up the pace, and Thomas went with it, following as he had been told to follow, without fear. As evening drew upon them, the companions came to a deep, still valley surrounded by tree-lined

T H O M A S   A N D   T H E   B O O K

slopes, and in the center was a house that had lights shining in its windows. Thomas was very glad to see that sight and hurried to the door, which stood open.

There stood a man in the habit of a monk, with a wise face and clear, bright eyes. He welcomed Thomas, led him inside to where a table had been laid with supper, and bade Thomas to say the words of blessing.

Of the beast there was no sign, but the monk seemed not to know of it, for he asked no questions. After he had eaten, Thomas spoke of the reason for his journey, and his host listened with bright eyes closed and said nothing until the end, when he looked straight at Thomas and said, "This is a great thing which you seek, but greater still is the mystery of your lineage, for you have heard the Voice of Tradition, and all that is to be revealed is already within you." But though Thomas questioned him closely as to the meaning of his words, he would say no more.

In the morning Thomas and his host made their devotions together and then Thomas went upon his way with food and water enough for the second day of his journey. Nor was he surprised to find the beast awaiting him upon the road, which they followed together as before until the midmost of the day, when they stopped to rest beneath a great tree that gave them shade from the heat of the sun.

As they sat thus, a rider came in sight along the road, coming at a great pace. When he saw where Thomas sat, with the beast silent beside him, he reined in his mount and got down. "Are you he who seeks the little book?" he asked.

"I am, indeed," answered Thomas, and he said again, eagerly, "Have you news of it?"

"Not I," said the stranger, "but I am sent to bring you gifts," and he gave Thomas a white cloth of very fine linen in which was wrapped a piece of cake and a little pot of tea and a cup from which to drink.

Thomas thanked the rider and asked who had sent these things.

"The Lady who lives within the Lake of Gold, hard by the resplendent Valley of Adventure."

"Then may I come with you to this Lady, that I may thank her for this fare?"

"She bade me say that you have no need to thank her, but that you must hasten onward and find that which you seek, for without you find it, she may no longer stay by the Lake of Gold in the Valley of Adventure. And she bade me say also that she is of your lineage, though you do not know her, and that through you, she shall continue."

With this, the messenger took leave of Thomas, who was suddenly aware that the beast was gone before him again on the road, and he followed where it lead, eagerly.

And so they went all the rest of that day until they came to a stretch of woodland that lay basking in the glint of the setting sun so that it seemed to glow from within. There the beast went apart amid the trees, and Thomas found himself alone. In the silence, he saw a light and heard the sound of a voice upraised in a song of praise to the Most High. Hurrying forward, he came to a clearing amid the trees and saw there a little chapel that lay almost hidden in a dip of the ground. From within the voice came, high and clear toned, exploring the shape of heaven through its harmony of sounds.

Thomas stood as though spellbound until the song was ended, joining only in the "amen" which he recognized. At this, there came forth from the chapel a strange figure dressed in rough cured skins and carrying a long staff of oak in his hands with which he both supported himself and found his way. For Thomas saw that he was blind.

"Friend," said the singer, "it is good that you have come at last." At this, Thomas was silent, for he knew with inward certainty that this man had waited his coming for a long time, and that he, Thomas, had always known this, although until this moment it had not been in the forefront of his mind.

"Yes," he replied, softly, "I have come, indeed. Is what I seek here?"

"Not here, not yet, but not far. Come you within and rest, and let he who accompanies you rest also," by which Thomas knew that he referred to the beast, and this was the first time that he realized that anyone save he could see the creature.

That night, as he lay upon the mattress of straw, scented with sweet herbs, Thomas thought that he dreamed. In his dream came many people, some that he knew and others that he did not. Many of them were odd, curious people, who seemed not altogether of this world—beautiful women in dresses of green leaves, and fair tall men with shining stars upon their brows. And each one that came to him said, "We are glad that you are seeking the book, for within it are our lives and our being. And we are all of your lineage, and you are the latest of our line."

And last of all came two figures who seemed older than all the rest, though in the prime of their lives. They bore about them such a dignity that, even in his dream, Thomas felt the power and awe that surrounded them. Had he been in a waking state, he felt that he would have fallen upon his knees before them. But they said, "We are your beginning, and we are your end, and in you is all that we are and all that we shall be, and upon you is the blessing of all who are to be." Then they were gone, and Thomas slept.

In the morning his host, the blind singer, woke Thomas and gave him fresh water to drink and set him upon his way through the wood, for of the beast there was no sign. Thomas walked all morning among the trees, listening to the chorus of birds, until he came at last to a clearing, in the midst of which was a fountain, which he recognized from the picture in the little book. Upon it was written many things that he afterwards remembered only in odd moments, though from that moment his life was changed.

Then there came from the trees a fair young man clad in white and red, who carried in one hand an apple, and in the other, the thing that Thomas sought. Thomas took the apple which was proffered first (not without a moment of doubt, remembering another apple), until he caught the merry eye of the youth and saw therein something that he recognized.

And when he had eaten the apple, he saw that the wood seemed familiar, and he remembered that it was near to his own small cell, at which thought wonder fell upon him, for he had walked there often in the past but had never seen either the fountain or the young man.

As though he knew what Thomas thought, the youth smiled and said, "It was always here, Thomas, though you saw it not. And I was always here also." Then he took up the little book that Thomas sought and gave it to him.

Thomas took it with a trembling hand. But the young man only smiled and said, "Go home, Thomas. Take pen and ink and copy out all that you find within this book that all who come thereafter may read it for themselves. This task you must complete in one year, and if you grow tired, you shall come here to the fountain and take of its water and of the fruits that grow hereabouts. Do this in memory of all who have been and all who will be, for thus is the mystery of their lineage made plain for all who would see."

Thomas bowed his head before the Voice of Tradition, and when he raised it again, he was alone.

Thomas went home to his cell and took up pen and ink and vellum as he had been told. He opened the little book, and with sharpened goose quill he wrote:

> Here is the Book of our Descent.
> Here begin the Terrors.
> Here begin the Mysteries.

SONG OF THE RETURNING

(1)

They have all gone, lamenting, under the hills,
lamenting for their lord who is lost,
hidden in the waste where the earth dried up
to the death of the grailless lands.

They have all gone under, into the raths
that are silent now, shut fast as a soul,
prisoned like their lord under lands of ice.

Mabon is lost and all is lost till the thaw,
when the ice breath shakes on the sickened land
and the king is set free from winter's boundless chains.

They have all gone, lamenting, under the land
to the place where the mothers of the race are born
where the myths of the grailless lands are born
to be spoken in whispers in the lightless realm.

(2)

He comes, the one who frees the waters,
and in his train comes spring—
the child of Modron reigns in splendor.

Bright as the light on the Radiant Brow
he stands at the aeon-gated city on the hill
with bow and quiver at his back.

And they who were gone, lamenting, lamenting,
come forth to dance in the morning light;
and the light falls long on the grailless lands
till the trees are adrift in rivers of light.

Mabon, Mabon we call you again,
free us from the prison of the iron gates,
free us again from winter's bite.

Mabon, Mabon, we call to you once more,
thrice we call you back through the open door
to dance on the grass at the water's gate.

For they who were lamenting, under the hills
return when you to dance on the hills,
and the children of the raths come forth into the wild.

And the sunlight dances in the grailless lands
and the moonlight flickers on the grailless lands—
for Mabon son of Modron has come out of the hills.

12

THE VISION OF THE MOTHER OF GOD

Most of the tales told by the great bard have little to do with the miracles of the Lord Christ. Yet I have noted before that he ever shows respect towards the beliefs of those who follow the Lord's teachings. In this tale there are many miraculous events, and it seems that the emperor Arthur himself bears witness to the glorious mysteries of the Blessed Saint Mary.

ou will have heard how, at the battle of Badon, Arthur carried a shield on which was painted an image of the Mother of God. And you will doubtless have been told that this device caused the tide of battle to turn in our favor, and that Arthur himself accounted for several hundred of the Saeson that day. ❧ I will not say that this story is a lie, simply that it has grown and changed in the telling. Such is the way with stories, especially after a battle such as Badon, where we routed the invaders at last and pushed them back to the very shores of the island. So it is, also, with men like Arthur, who have stories grow

on them like cloaks—until it is sometimes difficult to see the man inside at all!

Like all storytellers, I like to think I know the truth. In this instance, I want to set straight how this story about the shield came about and the effect it had upon what occurred on that glorious day at Badon.

The story begins when Arthur had not been king for very long. He had consolidated his power, to be sure, and gathered sufficient people to his side to make him the unquestioned force in the land. But he had yet to wear the crown officially or have the priests mumble their words of blessing over him. Indeed, he seemed unwilling to do so, declaring that he had yet to prove himself in battle or adventure.

It was for this reason that Arthur decided to visit the chapel in the White Forest. Certainly it had an unchancy reputation, and more than one story I could tell of it that would stir the hair on your heads. But we are speaking of Arthur here, and of Arthur we shall hear.

Having decided to go, he told only the queen and his closest advisors, who counseled him not to go at all, of course—or at least to take a large company of men with him. But Arthur could be stubborn when he wanted, and the more they insisted, the more determined he became to go forth alone. Finally he agreed to take a young body servant named Cahus to see to his needs. On the night before their departure, he gave the boy instructions to sleep in the hall and to ready the horses as soon as dawn cracked the edge of the sky.

It happened that in the night the boy began to dream. He dreamed that he had overslept and that the king had gone without him. And in his dream he saddled his own horse and rode as swiftly as he could into the White Forest. (I know not why it is called by that name, for it is a dark place, where many strange things lurk. Indeed, it is part of the great Wood that has existed from the beginning and will outlast us all.)

But I digress. In the dream Cahus arrived before a half-ruined building, which had a strange, wan light shining out from its single window. Thinking the king must have gone inside to rest, he dismounted and went in himself. There he saw a strange sight. The building was fitted out like a chapel, with an altar on which stood four elaborate gold candlesticks. In front of the altar lay the body of a richly dressed man, draped in a pall of silk.

The boy was puzzled by this sight, but even more by the absence of the king. Almost without thinking, he picked up one of the golden candlesticks and went outside again. He mounted his horse and was just about to ride on in search of Arthur, when he saw a huge ugly man approaching.

"Have you seen the king?" demanded the boy.

"I have not. But I have seen you and the golden relic that you have stolen from the White Chapel, and for that I shall repay you, unless you give it back at once."

Now, let me remind you that all these happenings were in the dream of the youth named Cahus. He, on being addressed thus roughly, suddenly found his pride and refused flatly to give up the candlestick. He tried to ride past the big man, who took out a large and wicked-looking knife and stuck it into him, just below the ribs on the left side.

Back in the hall at Carduil, the boy awoke with a scream. His cries soon awoke the rest of the household, including the king. When they arrived in the hall, they found the youth lying in a pool of blood, pinned down by the weight of a huge knife which was stuck into him on the left side, while in one hand he clutched a beautiful golden candlestick!

Before he died, Cahus told the king everything that had happened in the dream, and Arthur gave him his word that he would not only seek out the White Chapel, but that he would exact the full price for the young squire's death. When Cahus had breathed his last, Arthur called for his mount and set forth, forbidding anyone to follow him.

He rode all day until, as twilight was approaching, he found himself close to a ruined house in the heart of the forest. He dismounted, tethered his horse, and went in. There he saw everything just as Cahus had described it: the altar, the three remaining candlesticks, and the body of the man draped in a rich silken pall. Arthur knelt down and prayed for the soul of the departed man; then he went outside and looked about him for any sign of the ugly man. But the forest was silent, and darkness had begun to fall, so Arthur went back inside the ruined house and laid out his bed to sleep there in a corner.

Now, I cannot say whether the king dreamed or not, but here is how I have heard told what took place next. First, the king thought he heard two voices raised in anger, though he could nowhere see who it was that was speaking. One was a fair, kindly voice, while the other was rough and harsh. As Arthur listened, he learned that they were arguing over the soul of the dead knight, and from this he guessed that one voice belonged to an angel, and the other, to a demon.

Back and forth the quarrel raged, and then, after a little silence, a third voice spoke up. It seemed to the king that it must belong to the most beautiful woman anyone had ever seen. Soft and low, but with quiet authority, the voice said, "Depart, and cease this wrangling. For the soul of this worthy man belongs to us. My Son and I took him into our service five years since, and he has served us well."

"But," countered the rough voice, "before that, he was an evil man, a robber and a murderer in this very forest. It is not right that you take him from me."

"I do not take him from you," replied the beautiful voice. "He had already chosen to be in our service. If it were not so, he would have come willingly to you."

There was a long silence after that, and Arthur deemed that the demon had departed. Then, as he lay there in the ruined house, he heard the sound of a man chanting the words of the Holy Mass. He sat up and looked around, and all at once the house seemed filled with light, and he could see an aged hermit standing before the altar singing the words of the *Introit*. As the king looked on in wonder, he saw that on one side of the hermit stood a child, of no more than six or seven summers, who seemed to him the fairest child he had ever seen. And on the other side, seated in a beautiful chair, sat a woman whose face was so filled with light and joy that the king almost could not look upon it.

As he watched, the Lady called the Child to her and placed him upon her knees. In the voice which the king knew well from his dream, she said, "Sire, you are my Father and my Son, my Lord and my Guardian, and the Guardian of everyone."

Arthur was filled with wonder at this vision and so knelt down on the stone floor and joined in the responses of the Mass. And when it came to the *Offertorium*, he saw the Lady offer the Child to the hermit, who in turn raised him in his hands above the altar. At this there came through the window behind the altar a spear of light so bright that the king was momentarily blinded. When he could see again, only the hermit stood there, with bowed head, and of the Lady and the Child there was no sign.

Shaken, Arthur remained for a long time kneeling, until at last the hermit helped him to stand and led him outside into the fresh morning air. When Arthur had come back somewhat to himself, the hermit uttered these mysterious words: "King Arthur, this vision has been granted to you in token of the great adventure of the Grail, which has yet to happen, but which will change the story of this land forever. Go now, and in the battle that is to come, remember what you have seen."

Arthur could find nothing to say by way of answer to these words, but solemnly took his leave of the hermit and turned his horse towards Carduil. He had traveled only a little way, when he saw standing in his path a huge and ugly man, whom he guessed at once was the same who had slain the boy Cahus in so strange a manner. Arthur drew his sword so as to be ready and urged his mount forward.

The big man did not move. His face was grim, and when the King was close to him, he said, "King Arthur, you have in your possession that which belongs to me, and to my brother whose tomb your servant robbed."

"As to that," replied the King sternly, "I have no wish to keep the candlestick. But there was no need to kill my squire for it. That I cannot forgive."

"No more can I forgive the theft of the candlestick," replied the big man.

"Then let us settle this matter once and for all," said Arthur, "since we both have grievances of the other."

This said, Arthur got down from his horse, and the two warriors dressed their shields to each other. The big man hefted a huge axe in his hand, while Arthur attacked with his sword, and the two fought furiously until at last the king got the better of his opponent and slew him. When the big man fell to the earth, the blood that gushed from him was black and smoked, so they say, and in that smoke, his body melted away. From which, Arthur knew that he had been fighting a demon.

Well, the king rode back to Carduil without further adventure. When he was safely within the walls of the great fortress, he called to him a certain artisan and asked him to paint an image of the Mother of God on the inside of his shield.

That was the shield he bore at Badon, and as you all know, he fought as bravely as any man ever did on that day and led us all to victory over the Saeson. It is said that whenever his arm grew tired or his spirits sank, the king looked upon the face of the image of the Mother of God within his shield and fought on renewed.

As to the mysterious words of the hermit concerning the Grail, that must wait for another night to be told, for there are as many stories of Arthur as there are days in the week and months in the year and years in ages of ages, and even I do not know them all.

SONG OF PELLES THE GRAIL KING

"Listen," he told us, "to the voice of the wind
as it unloads its burden of meaning
without which you cannot grow."
The wind groaned across the wards,
shook fists in the faceless windows,
boomed in the towers where we lay.

He, in his stone chair, the iron crown
Deep on his brows, stared at the white edge
Of the world with eyes alight
and saw nothing but shadows of his life.
A prey to dreams beyond hope,
he knelt in the dust to beg for time.

GALAHAD AND THE SHIP OF THE GRAIL

13
GALAHAD AND
THE HOLY THINGS

Of all the stories in the bundle I discovered among the dust and cobwebs of the scriptorium, this one most moves me. I know but little of the heroes of the Round Table, save that they lived at a time far more distant than tales such as this one would have us believe, and that the story of the quest for the cup of Jesus Christ—though that seems only one of the vessel's marvels—stretches back to a most ancient time, long before the recollection of even the oldest tales related here. Whatever the truth may be, this story is most human in its description of the love of father for son and son for father, a love as deep as the sinful passion that harrowed the great knight Lancelot. ❧ In the ancient book written by the Lord Taliesin, these things are told differently, and much more is said concerning the mysterious ship in which the two men sailed. There it is said that this craft was built from timbers of the Great Wood of which the bard speaks so often, and that it sailed not only the waters of the ocean, but the sea of time as well, passing down the ages until it arrived in the time of Arthur, when the mysteries here described took place. This seems, then, one of the tales added to the collection by a later hand than that *of the little monk who was Taliesin's scribe. But of this I know nothing more and would let the tale speak for itself.*

It was Maytime when Galahad came, his red armor gleaming amid the bright blossoms like blood upon the petals of a rose. His coming was mysterious, ushered into the hall by an old withered man leaning upon a stout ash staff as the Round Table fellowship sat at meat together. Wonder was upon every face in that place of many wonders, as the old man silently led the beautiful youth to the Siege Perilous, that seat at the table in which it was said no man might sit but the one appointed to achieve the greatest adventure of all—the finding of the Grail.

This act alone foretold strange and wondrous events. But while the knights fell silent, glancing towards each other and to where the king sat in his great chair, another and greater wonder befell. For suddenly there was a great crashing and crying of elemental forces. All the wooden shutters banged shut, and the great doors to the hall were sealed so that none might enter or go out. Then a strong wind arose that blew throughout the hall and guttered all the candles. In the hushed darkness, one of the windows flung open with a crash, and into the dimness there shone a ray of light brighter by far than any candle flame. Within the ray all there espied a thing—a beauteous and radiant cup that floated above their heads, emitting a power such as none there had ever felt before.

Every man began to look at his neighbor, and it is said that what they saw was the truth about each one, so that many dropped their gaze or fell to looking again at the bright wonder that floated serenely above them. Then the aged man, he who had guided the red armored youth to his place, spoke up. "Here begin the mysteries of the Grail," he said. "Now begins the time of testing and of sorrow. For many shall go forth this day, but few shall return, and fewer still shall discover what they seek. This youth is named Galahad. I recommend him unto you all."

As he spoke these words, the light that shone from the Grail grew dim and then disappeared. Light and movement returned to the hall of the Round Table, the doors and windows were unsealed, and men sat blinking in wonder at what had transpired. Some might even have believed themselves to have fallen asleep and to have dreamed the events, but that the pale youth in his iron red mail was sitting as before in the Siege Perilous and there was besides a sweet savor in the air as of summer flowers or the incense that scented the great basilica in the city below.

Into the silence and uneasiness broke the voice and figure of Sir Gawain: "My lords and my friends, hear me! Such wonders as we have seen this day! Let all know that I make this vow: that I shall not rest, nor cease from searching, until I have discovered the true meaning of these things."

Many there murmured assent, while others sprang from their places and cried aloud that they, too, would set forth at once in search of the bright mystery. Only Arthur sat still and silent, sunk in thought. And when at last he spoke—all there turning at once to hear him—it was with heavy words: "My lords, your courage and your ardor does you credit. Yet I fear that I shall not see many of you again, and that this may well be the ending of our great fellowship. Yet I wish you well and send you forth with my blessing." Having said which, the king arose and walked slowly from the hall, leaving many to wonder at his words, while others sat and thought upon their own mortality.

Within the week every one of the fellowship then present had set forth, led by the bold-speaking Gawain. They went by all the roads leading from the city, and if at first they set forth with high hearts and in goodly companies, they were soon silent and, as days turned to weeks and one or another turned aside upon a different path, increasingly alone. The chronicle of their deeds has been told before and will be told again. Many who had lived and fought for the good of both land and king meet their doom upon that quest. Precious few were chosen to know the mysteries of the Grail.

Gawain himself, who was ever light of purpose, soon turned aside to other things, and the story tells of him no more. Instead it speaks of four knights: Perceval, Bors, Galahad, and Lancelot. These four came closer than all the rest to the heart of the mystery, and each of their stories would take a night to tell. Here

I would tell only of two: Galahad and Lancelot, of how they met upon the road and what transpired because of that meeting.

Lancelot had been long upon the quest when he came one day to the shore of the sea and saw there a strange ship with silent red sails on which were emblazoned a bright picture—the Grail itself with a sunburst around it. In the boat sat a single figure, pale bright hair spilling over his travel-worn red clothes. At sight of the mail-clad figure on the shore, the man on the boat lifted his hand in greeting and beckoned to Lancelot to join him. Recognizing the youth who had come on that fateful day and who had sat in the Perilous Siege unscathed, Lancelot dismounted, and leaving his horse to wander free, went aboard the strange ship. At once, a wind sprang up, and the sail filled, driving the craft from the shore and out into the ocean.

Once Lancelot would have questioned a vessel that set forth without benefit of crew, but so many strange events had dogged his path since leaving Camelot, he no longer even thought to ask. Instead he looked long and straightly at his companion—and saw there himself mirrored. "How is it that we are so alike?" he asked his companion in puzzlement.

"Do you not know?" came the quiet answer.

As Lancelot heard the words, it seemed that he did know. His mind went back to a time, many years since, when he had rescued a girl from a bath of boiling water, in which she had been set by dire spells, and how that same night he had received a message that seemed to come from the queen, summoning him to her rooms in a nearby castle. How sweet that night had seemed, until, upon waking, he discovered by his side, not the queen, but the girl he had but lately rescued.

His mind returned to the moment of that waking and then as swiftly back to the serious face of the youth before him. "You are Elaine's child."

"I am."

"Then, you are my . . . son."

A trembling began in Lancelot's limbs. It seemed impossible that he had not known it before, had not seen it writ large upon the boy's face that first time when he had entered the hall of the Round Table. Tears he had not known were in him clouded his eyes, and he reached out blindly to Galahad.

If both wept that day, I know it not or will not speak of it. But it is certain that they had many things to say to each other as the mysterious ship drove on through the sea. Perhaps Galahad spoke of his childhood among the sisters of Amesbury, where his mother had sent him to learn the ways of prayer and of the mystery he was destined to seek. For the quest for the Grail had been his task from birth, and he knew of no other. As for Lancelot, whether he spoke of the love that tore his very soul, I shall not say. Only that in the days that followed, the two men talked of many things, and they each found fellowship and love in the other.

Then, one night, Lancelot had a dream. He dreamed that he stood outside the door to a chapel from which radiant beams of light shone forth, and that as he looked within, he saw an aged priest celebrating Holy Mass. As the priest came to the Offering of the Host, Lancelot thought that he struggled to hold aloft the body of a man who bled from hands and feet and brow. He rushed forward to help but was struck down by a breath as of fire, while a Voice spoke in his head that said: "Not for you the way of the Grail! You have chosen another path."

Lancelot awoke with tears upon his cheeks and told Galahad of his dream. The young knight was silent for a long time, but at length he said: "My noble father, I think you know the meaning of this dream. It is a thought that has been in my mind since we met upon this voyage, and already it is a cause of great sorrow to me, though I know it must be so, and that there is no gainsaying the destiny that is laid upon us both. For I believe the time is fast approaching when our fortune must take us separate ways."

As though his words had ushered in a change, the sails of the boat luffed and it turned about in the water, making for land. There, in the distance, but growing swiftly larger, was a castle set atop a cliff. Bright light came from it as though it were built of sun and air. Lancelot and Galahad looked upon it together and said nothing more to each other until the keel ground upon the shore.

Then Galahad rose and, placing a hand upon each of his father's great shoulders, looked deep into his eyes. "Though we meet never again in this world, yet am I glad that we have shared these days together."

Lancelot smiled. "It is small enough time for a father to know his son."

Galahad smiled back but said no more. And though he took leave of Lancelot with love and warmth, yet it seemed that his eyes ever turned towards the guiding star of the castle, and his thoughts were already upon the task that lay before him.

So the two knights, father and son, parted. Nor did they indeed meet again in this life. Lancelot watched his son walk alone up the path towards the castle, never once looking back. As he watched, the sails above his head filled again with the breath of air, and the ship moved away from the shore. Lancelot's last glimpse was of the castle, shining like a star on the headland far above, and of a sound which seemed to him like the note of a great bell sounding forth into the dimming day.

That night he dreamed again, and the dream seemed to him a gift from the Grail itself. For as he lay, restless in the boat that carried him ever further from the place his heart longed to be, he saw again the chapel from which he had been turned away. And there he saw his son, clad now in raiment of white, holding before him a mighty spear, while before him stood a man whose face was all of light, and who held the vessel of all heart's desire in his hands and offered Galahad to drink.

With all his soul in his eyes, the young knight took what he had sought from the day of his birth. In his dream, Lancelot could not bear to look upon the face of his son as he drew back and fell upon his knees, then sank slowly to the ground. Two other knights, whom Lancelot recognized as Perceval and Bors, held the body of their comrade and laid it down upon the floor of the chapel. Then a great pealing of bells and voices broke out, waking Lancelot from sleep. In that moment it seemed that he could still hear the sound, which faded as he woke, cold and alone on the ship, his cheeks wet with his own salt tears.

Yet these were tears not of sorrow, but of great gladness, for he felt the joy of his son's achievement as though he had been there to witness it in person. Even though Lancelot himself returned to Camelot and to the love that had become a canker in his soul, yet the bright blessing of the Grail, perceived by him through the love of his son, awakened in him an answering joy. As he turned his mind towards Camelot and the queen, his heart was lighter, and the memory of Galahad was bright within him.

GRAIL

(I)
This cup
holds light
like liquid,
burning holes
in the heart.

This icon
signifies
the birth
of truth
in a dead heart.

This light,
illuminating,
wraps around
the dark.

(II)
From the edges of space
light, gathered up,
is centered
into a single drop.

It blossoms in the Grail,
becoming more real;
hangs in the treetops
like a fatherless child,

waiting for someone
passing,
to take it home.

(III)
I have stood at the table
of the Winter King,
eaten of the food
set before me;
shared in the goodness
that was mine to share.

Wherefore now do I stand
in the chill night
on the wintry moor,
bereft of speech
as the Cauldron Born.

(IV)
I have tasted
food of the Grail.
Fool no more,
I walk the world
searching again
for the door
that opened
once before,
admitting me to
the garden beyond.

14

COLLEN AND THE LORD
OF THE MOUND

hen I first began to read and copy the stories gathered here, I found myself wondering often how the great bard regarded those who, like myself, worship the Lord Christ. Then I came upon the story that follows, which is written in the characteristic script of the little monk and contains a fragment of a song by the bard himself. It is a tale that deals with the clash between the two beliefs—the way of Christ and the older path that Taliesin followed. This theme in itself would seem reason enough to include it, but it also seems to me to deal with matters not unconnected with the other tales the bard tells.

wynn ap Nudd had ruled over the People of the Mound for more than a thousand years, for longer, indeed, than he could remember. The doings of the folk outside the Mound never troubled him. From time to time he heard of a new king who had come to rule over the Lands Above, and sometimes heroes (an annoying breed) found their way into the Lands Beneath and caused him some slight trouble, but by

and large he remained unconcerned about mortal men and their ways. That is, until the day when he noticed that there were fewer of his own folk at the court under the Mound, and that several inexplicable cracks had appeared in the roof of his palace, cracks that should not have been there, since the fabric of the place, like all the works of the Lands Beneath the Land, was intended to last forever.

Filled as he was with years and wisdom, it did not take Gwynn long to discover that the two occurrences had something to do with the race of men. So he sent for his wiliest and most trusted adviser, who was at least as old, if not older than Gwynn himself, and demanded an explanation.

What he heard was so disturbing that it caused Gwynn to feel seriously perplexed for the first time in several hundred years. It seemed that a new kindred of men had come to live in the Lands Above who were followers of a new god. There had been such before, of course, but recently a surprising number of the folk of the Lands Above had begun to follow this new god and, as a result, had begun to doubt the existence of the People of the Mound and ignore the customs and observances due to them. Not many, it was true, had fallen seriously from the old ways, but enough shrines and wells were being neglected to cause some of their incumbents to fade or, in some cases, to vanish utterly. This lapse was also the cause of the cracks that had appeared so ominously in the roof of the royal chamber.

Gwynn thought about what he had been told for several days. Then word reached him that one of his people, a friendly and unassuming marsh sprite, had encountered one of these new sorts of priests and had been knocked into a mud pit when he had tried to stop the man from building a causeway across his part of the marsh. So angered was Gwynn by this report that he decided to summon one of the new believers to answer for this crime, and forthwith sent word by a trusted messenger to a place only a mile or so distant in the Lands Above, where a community of monks had set up a dwelling of some size.

The man he picked upon for this confrontation was named Collen. He had a reputation for wisdom and holiness surprising in one as yet still young, and many thought him marked for higher things, though Collen himself chose to live his life independently of those who kept trying to persuade him to take office in the Church. But he could not prevent the people from bringing their problems to him in spite of his humility—indeed, he knew it would have been wrong to try. So he was not surprised when a rather curious looking creature appeared at the entrance to his cell and asked if he would come to see his master and help settle a dispute.

I am most excited to read this account, for our records relate that Collen was often found at Ynys Witrin and that he lived in this very abbey for a time. Abbot Thomas himself has written of this great man, whose wisdom was indeed, as is described here, of a wondrous kind.

Collen got up immediately and followed the man along the path that led away from the monastery towards the great hill known as the Tor. It was only when they had been traveling for some time that Collen realized they were climbing the side of this ancient hill, where he knew there to be no human dwellings. So he stopped and asked his guide who his master was. Next moment, there was a quivering and shaking in the air, and Collen found himself standing in a vast hall, roofed with a golden canopy held up by fantastic pillars. Brilliant tapestries hung from its walls, while on every side were rich ornaments and treasures such as any man would find hard to imagine.

Collen stood, leaning on his staff and looking around in mild amazement. But the harder he looked, the more insubstantial the place seemed, as though it were not really there and might fade or vanish at any moment. The pillars, though beautiful, were formed from naturally striated rock; the walls, where they showed through the ornate tapestries, were of rough hewn stone. When Collen raised his eyes to the roof, he saw there not only the glimmer of stars—though somehow under the earth—but also the vast and heavy stones that covered the place.

So busy was he in looking at all this that Collen was not at first aware of the people. But gradually it dawned upon him that the great hall in which he stood was filling with strange and beautiful beings the likes of which Collen had never dreamed existed. There were tall and stately women, whose raiment seemed made of tree bark or leaves or living water, and whose hair stirred as though to an unfelt breeze, and striking men with a greenness about their skin like loam, their clothing seemingly of earth and moss and still growing leaves. In the eyes of these fair beings was a glow that spoke of a life force so strong as to make most human folk seem like dead things.

As Collen stared, so they stared back: seeing a small, solid man with once black hair now pied with gray, dressed in a plain white robe and leaning on a rough hewn staff. Bright black eyes regarded them steadily and without fear—something most there were unaccustomed to in men.

Collen's scrutiny was broken by a great voice that suddenly boomed out: "Welcome, child of the Lands Above, to the Lands Below!"

Collen turned and saw a tall splendid being seated on a golden throne that was carved over the back and arms with a hundred laughing, smiling, grimacing, snarling faces. The being was dressed in a great cloak of animal skins, and under his fine garments, rich red gold glittered at neck and wrists. His wild hair and beard had a hint of green about them and gleamed with raw energy; his eyes were wellsprings of secret knowledge and the delight of life. Two hounds crouched at his feet, each one white as cloud—save for their ears, which were red as blood. They looked upon the visitor from the world of men with their own bright intelligence.

"Welcome, Collen," said the personage on the throne, "to my kingdom. Let us sit and eat together and afterwards talk for a while."

"I will be glad to talk with you," answered Collen, "but first I would know with whom I speak."

The King of the Lands Beneath threw back his great head and laughed. "I have many names, and one is as good as another. In your world, I am known as Gwynn ap Nudd, or Avallach, or as the Fisher."

With this Collen had to be content. Instantly, a table was set before him and rich food and wine laid upon it. But of these he would have none, having a good idea where he was and knowing the prohibitions about eating the food and drink of that place. Instead, he asked simply for some water; and though Gwynn frowned at this, he made no move to force his guest, but bade the table be removed and called for music. When the strains of a harp filled the hall, he bade Collen's chair to be brought close to him and said, "I would learn something of your ways. Tell me of your life in the Lands Above and of the new god you follow."

If Collen was surprised, he did not show it. With a smile, he launched into an account of the birth, death, and return to life of the one whom he called the Son of Light, who had dwelled among men as a man but who had shown by certain wondrous deeds that he was more than a man.

Gwynn ap Nudd listened without interrupting and with great attention, and afterwards asked several questions. At last he said, "You profess to follow your god in loving all things and all men, yet you and your kind make war on me and mine. How do you explain this?"

Collen replied, "We make war upon no men. You are not men at all, nor are you part of my God's creation. Therefore, we have no need to acknowledge you. As far as we are concerned, you do not exist."

And though this was said politely and without anger, the Lord of Annwn rose abruptly to his feet, spilling wine from the rich golden cup he held. "It is as I thought!" he cried. "You seek our ending—we who were here before your foolish race were spawned upon the earth; we who have guarded and tended the Lands Above since the beginning. You seek to hasten our passing. Yet, when we are gone, there will be an end to many things that you would as soon not lose. The power of earthly kings will wane, and the land itself will grow sick."

"Better that it should be so," answered Collen calmly, "than that men should worship false gods or the spirits of river and tree."

The King of the Otherworld snorted in disgust. "I see that we have nothing to say to each other, mortal. Whatever you may say or do, we shall be here when you have long become dust, you and all your kind. Now go!" He waved his hand in dismissal, and at once Collen found himself standing alone on the summit of the Tor in a keen wind.

Collen addressed the empty air: "All this world is beautiful, King of Annwn, with or without your help."

The only answer was a faint tremor in the earth as of a great door slamming shut in the Lands Beneath.

But this was not to be the last that Collen saw of the Lord of Annwn. A year passed in the Lands Above and the seasons went by, until once again winter held the land in thrall. Collen continued to work in the fields around the monastery and to walk the countryside speaking to any who would listen about his God. The little community grew slowly until it held as many as twenty monks and gave shelter to travelers who passed that way. Then, one morning, as Collen sat deep in meditation in his small cell, there came in at the window a wren that cocked its head on one side and addressed the little monk in a bright, hard voice: "Collen, the Lord of Annwn bids you visit him again."

Collen looked at the bird and said, "Tell your master I will come, but in my own time." When the messenger had flown away, Collen finished his orisons, took up his staff and a flask of holy water, and set out across the frozen fields and water meadows towards the Tor. When he stood at last on the summit, he knocked with his staff on the hard earth and called, "Lord of Annwn, I am here."

At once there was a swirl of movement in the air, and once again Collen found himself standing in the great underground hall with its pillars and tapestries and crowds of brightly garbed folk. And there as before was the imposing figure of Gwynn ap Nudd with his two red-eared hounds at his feet.

This time, he did not offer Collen food or drink but spoke directly of the matter that had caused him to summon the monk again. "Once, long ago—as you measure time in the Lands Above—there were wise and unbiased judges upon whom any creature could call for any reason. Now it seems that all such men have departed, and there are none to be found who will make peace between those who seek it. Therefore, I have called you, Collen, for despite the differences between us, I believe you to be an honest man without fear. Will you therefore act as judge in a matter that troubles me greatly?"

Collen answered, "If there is anything that I can honestly do, that will I do."

"Then listen, and observe," said Gwynn ap Nudd. He then told Collen how there lived a girl of surpassing beauty named Creiddelyadd, daughter of Llud Silver Hand. She was loved by Gwythyr, son of Greidyawl, the Lord of Summer, and by Gwynn himself who, because he was the stronger, raised an army against Gwythyr and took him prisoner, along with the maiden. Now all this had taken place in the time of Uther Pendragon, the father of the Ymerawdwr Arthur, whose wife Igraine was the sister of Creiddelyadd. When he heard of the matter, Uther went with his own warriors and took back Gwythyr and the girl from Gwynn ap Nudd. Then he sent the girl back to her father. There the matter stood.

"But I was unable to forget the beautiful Creiddelyadd," said the Lord of Annwn, "and it seemed to me right that she should belong to me because I am the strongest. Therefore, since that time, I have summoned Gwythyr ap Greidyawl to fight with me once every year on May Eve. And though we have fought on that day ever since, neither has won the victory."

While he listened, it seemed to Collen that he saw all that was described: the beautiful maiden, the Lord of Annwn on a night black horse, with armor that seemed to absorb the light, in combat with Gwythyr, who rode a horse the color of sunlight and wore armor of gold—two mighty champions who fought with primal strength but could not overcome each other for all their striving.

As the Lord of Annwn finished his tale Collen was suddenly back again in the hall of the Lands Beneath and blinked in the subtly shifting light.

"How say you to this matter?" demanded Gwynn ap Nudd.

"I am no druid, Lord of Annwn, nor have I any right to judge such as you," answered Collen. "Yet, I will give my opinion as to how this matter may best be resolved." He drew himself up. "It may be that I am a foolish mortal who has no understanding of such things, yet I believe I see a greater parable here than the love of two mighty beings for one woman. Fair indeed is the lovely Creiddelyadd, and mighty indeed are you, my Lord of the Lands Beneath. And so, too, is the might and strength of the Lord Gwythyr ap Greidyawl. But in your striving, I see a pattern: You are like the Winter and your opponent is like the Summer, and you each strive for possession of the Lady of Spring. Perhaps you each desire lordship over the rest of the year, for I have heard such things are sometimes so in the Lands Beneath. But all of this is merely a tale to me, and you are no more real than the shadow cast by a tree at midday.

"So, I say to you, Lord of Annwn, that there are laws immutable to such as you; and that the most immutable of all is the law that says that season must be followed by season, according to the pattern of creation. And I see now that I was wrong to say that you were not a part of my God's making, for you are so, indeed—even if you do not really exist—and as such, you are subject to certain laws yourself."

Collen paused, while Gwynn looked at him with open astonishment. Then Collen said: "This, then, is my judgment, for which you have asked me: You shall struggle for victory in this fight every year as you have already striven, until the coming of Doomsday. Only then shall this question finally be resolved, though how, I cannot say. And now, I would be gone from here, and may the blessing of the Son of Light be upon you and upon all here."

As he said these words, Collen took out from within his robe a little bottle of holy water and sprinkled a few drops on the ground. At which there came again a crash like a great door slamming shut, and the monk found himself standing again on the summit of the Tor, with the great voice of Gwynn ap Nudd ringing in his ears.

"Collen, your judgment is wise, though harsh, but you have shown me that there may yet be peace between the followers of your god and those of the old way, despite all that is between us."

Collen smiled as he walked down the sloping sides of the Tor, along the old path that men still called the Maze, and back to his little cell at the monastery that men were beginning to call Glastonbury. As he went, he sang a hymn to his God that told of the beauty of the world and of all creation.

As for Gwynn ap Nudd, he has not been seen as often as at one time, and there are few now who remember him, or his like. But I made a song that put words in the Lord of the Mound's own mouth:

> I am called an enchanter
> I am Gwynn the son of Nudd
> The lover of Creiddelyadd, daughter of Llud.
> This is my horse Carngrwn
> The terror of the field; he will not
> Let me parlay with you; when bridled
> He is restless; he is impatient
> To go to my home on the Tawe.

WASTELAND HEALED

The year turns over,
bright light after gold.

Shafts spring from the Grail,
bending sight.

We are dazzled—
but only so that

In the moment of dazzlement,
we may see, clipped close,

the unfurled pattern of the year:
in which, attending, we say:

The Grail will rise,
the Wasteland's healed;

Our part is to wonder,
to preserve life's law.

Part IV
FUGITIVE TALES

15

THE HOSTEL OF THE QUICKEN TREES

The story that follows might seem to have no part in the others related by the great bard were it not for a note that I found attached to it, written in the spidery hand of the scribe who I have come to believe collected these scrolls in the first place. It says, simply: "Fionn is another name for Taliesin, for both possess the White Wisdom." What this wisdom may be I know not, unless it be the visionary gift of which the bard frequently speaks. Could it be that in some mysterious way the two men shared each other's souls? I have heard it said that such is possible, though it lies outside my understanding and rightly belongs to the belief of the pagans. However, I cannot help but feel some curiosity regarding this matter, despite the risk to my own immortal soul. The story itself is a strange one, and after I first read it, I passed more than one dream-ridden night.

 ost would agree that of all the warriors who served with Fionn mac Cumhail in the Fianna, Diarmuid O'Duibhne was the greatest. No task was too great for him; no feat of arms or course of hunting too hard for

him to try. And he had besides a face and form that women loved, which caused great sorrow among the Fianna in times to come. Still in all, while Diarmuid rode with them, the Fianna were the most unbeatable men in Ireland.

The coming of Diarmuid was this wise: As a boy he went with other boys to be trained by the great warrior woman, Mongfinn, but in time he came to leave her and, with his youthful companions, made for Allmu of the White Walls to take service with Fionn mac Cumhail—that old, great warrior who was possessed also of so much wisdom. How many heroes are there who are poets also, or who command the wisdom of the Old Ones who live in the Hollow Hills? Yet, such was Fionn. Small wonder that above half the warriors in the land of Erin sought to follow him. The Fianna, these fighters were called. They were the best of the best, but Diarmuid would, one day, outshine them all.

It was ever my belief that the Fianna were the stuff of legends, yet here the bard speaks of them as if they were real men. Many folk in this time speak of Arthur and his fellowship in this wise, too; yet in the writings of the Lord Taliesin is ample proof of their reality. Thus I have learned to see what truth can lie hidden behind the mists of time, which makes all seem unreal where once hearts beat and bone and sinew strove within the world.

On the way to Fionn's hall, Diarmuid and his companions came to a ford in the river. By its banks was an old woman who begged them to carry her across. All of the boys refused, fearing to dirty their clothes with the mud of the river. Only Diarmuid took pity on the old woman and waded across the river with her in his arms. When he reached the other side, his companions having gone ahead without him, he found that the old woman he carried had transformed into a great shining figure that he knew for one of the Lordly Ones from the Otherworld, known in that place as Tir na nOg.

The shining woman smiled at him and said, "Diarmuid O'Duibhne, you are a good son and will do many great deeds; and for the goodness you had to myself today, I promise that no woman shall ever refuse you, nor be able to resist your looks. And I tell you also that you have not seen the last of this place, for here shall another feat be attempted, one that shall be remembered." And with these words still hanging in air, of a sudden there was no one there at all.

So Diarmuid went on to Allmu of the White Walls. There Fionn saw him and with his Thumb of Wisdom knew what had occurred and that the old woman Fionn had carried across the river had been the Battle Goddess Morrighan herself. But about her prophecy he felt troubled doubts, which were to prove well founded later on.

I have read that the terrible warrior Fionn Mac Cumhail was able to see the future by biting his thumb. Taliesin himself, stories say, burned his thumb on the hot liquid bubbling in the cauldron of another terrible witch. When he put his thumb into his mouth to soothe the pain, he gained the knowledge that made him all wise. Can this be part of the mystery that links the two men?

As to the prophecy that Diarmuid would come to that ford again, this is the way that it came about: Many years later, Fionn fought a battle against the King of Lochlan and slew him and all his sons, save one only—Midac, whom he took into his own house and afterwards gave lands on the coast of Ireland. But in all that time, never a word of thanks did Fionn have from Midac, who continued in secret to plot against his benefactor.

One day, it chanced that the Fianna were hunting in the hills to the west of Allmu and, as sometimes happened, Fionn and some of his men became separated from their fellows who were following the track of a boar towards Cnoc Fianna. As they went, they saw a tall and handsome warrior coming towards them. When he saw that it was Midac, Fionn greeted him cheerfully enough. The King of Lochlan's son smiled smoothly (though there were some among the Fianna who knew his true color) and invited the hunting party to sup with him at the Hostel of the Quicken Trees, which was nearby.

To this courtesy Fionn readily agreed and commanded that certain of the band, Oisin and Diarmuid, Fodla and Caoilte mac Ronan, and his own youngest son, Fiachna, together with his foster-brother Innsa, should remain behind until the remainder of the hunt came up with them. Then Fionn and Goll mac Morna, and Conan Maol, and the rest, rode after Midac to the Hostel of the Quicken Trees.

The hostel was a fair and beautiful building, with bright intricate carvings on the wood of its uprights and a fresh thatch that shone in the sunlight like gold. All around it grew quicken trees, with berries full and red upon them. Fionn and his men followed Midac within and were amazed at the richness they beheld: fine hangings on every wall, soft couches to rest on, and a bright roaring fire in the hearth to warm them.

"Certainly you have done well by yourself," said Fionn to Midac, but when he looked around, their host was nowhere to be seen. "Is this not a strange thing? And no servants to be seen either?" he asked.

"There is something stranger than that," said Goll. "For but a moment since the walls were hung with fine stuffs, and now they seem but rough planks through which the wind blows."

"And there is something else strange," said Fiachna. "When we came in, there were seven doors, but now there is only one, and that is closed tight."

"What is more," added Conan, "these soft couches we were sitting upon seem to have become as hard as the earth—perhaps because they are!"

Seeing treachery and magic thus revealed, the Fianna made to rise and break out of the hall—only to find that they could not move, but were anchored fast to the floor as though with bands of iron.

Then Fionn put his Thumb of Wisdom between his teeth and groaned aloud: "Now is the treachery of Midac mac Lochlan revealed," he said, "for I see a great host coming against us, led by Sinsar of the Battles, and his son Borba the Haughty, and coming with them are the three sons of the King of Torrent. It is the last named whose spells hold us here, and only the scattering of their blood on the floor will set us free. But of that there is little chance."

Then the men of the Fianna sent up the war cry, the *Diord Fionn*, and so loud was their cry that Fiachna and Innsa heard it and hurried down to the Hostel of the Quicken Trees to discover what was amiss. When they heard what had come to pass, the two young warriors felt their battle rage come upon them and at once said they would defend the hostel at whatever cost, making their stand at a ford nearby that the enemy host must needs cross before they came to the hostel where Fionn and his men were imprisoned.

Meanwhile, the host that was coming to destroy Fionn had made camp at a few miles' distance. It occurred to one of Midac's chieftains that if he went with his own men and slew Fionn and brought the head back to his master, great fortune would be his. So he set off and came to the ford where Innsa and Fiachna waited. There ensued a great combat in which Innsa fell to Midac's chieftain, and Fiachna in turn slew him along with so many of his warriors that only a handful returned to Midac.

Fiachna buried Innsa in a shallow grave and bore the news of his death and the slaughter of their enemies to Fionn, who wept for the death of his foster son. But still he and the Fianna were held fast, nor would Fiachna abandon them and go for the rest of the war band.

Meanwhile, another chieftain of Midac's, named Ciaran, fell to wondering why his brother and their men had not returned and set forth in search of them. When they came to the ford, they found it choked with the bodies of the slain and Fiachna waiting to meet them.

Then there followed one of those combats that live in the memory of men long after. Fiachna held the ford alone against many dozens of attackers. At the end of it, only one man escaped to take the news to Midac.

He in turn became so enraged that he gathered a part of his own men and made for the ford, where he found Fiachna still leaning on his sword and bleeding from many wounds. When Midac saw all the bodies of his men and how they made a wall of dead in the stream, he flung himself forwards and engaged the young hero in single combat.

Meanwhile, Oisin, Fodla, and Diarmuid had been waiting for word from Fiachna. When none came, Diarmuid and Fodla decided to go down to the Hostel of the Quicken Trees to find out what was amiss, while Oisin went after the rest of the war band. As they were nearing the place, they heard the sounds of battle and began to run, emerging at the place in time to see Fiachna, hard pressed, give way at last before the fury of Midac's attack. Without pausing in his stride, Diarmuid flung his spear a great throw that took Midac in the breast and laid him on his back, though not before Midac had struck a blow that gave Fiachna his death.

Then, as Fodla gave battle to the rest of Midac's men, Diarmuid struck off the head of Fionn's enemy and carried it to the door of the hostel. When he found what had occurred there, he groaned aloud but said that he and Fodla would hold the ford against all comers until Oisin returned with the rest of the Fianna. "And if the sons of the King of Torrent come hither while we wait, you may be sure you shall be set free the sooner," he vowed.

Diarmuid returned to the ford and found that Fodla had driven off the few remaining men of Midac's war band. Fodla was so exhausted with fighting that once he saw Diarmuid, he fell into a deep sleep there on the bank amid all the dead. Diarmuid covered him with a cloak and left him to rest undisturbed.

Now, at last, the main body of the host that Midac had gathered, namely that of the three sons of the King of Torrent, came to the ford, and there for long hours Diarmuid held them at bay, single handed, not liking to wake the sleeping Fodla. But in time, the noise of the battle did awaken him, and little pleased he was that he had missed so much of the fight.

The two warriors together drove back the enemy with dreadful slaughter. In the end, Diarmuid himself slew all three of the king's sons and took their heads. Then while Fodla chased off the rest, Diarmuid went again to the Hostel of the Quicken Trees and sprinkled the blood on the doorstep and the earth within. But though Fionn and his men were able to move, they still had no strength. Fionn told Diarmuid that they would not be able to fight before morning, when their strength would return.

So once again Diarmuid returned alone to the ford, and there he and Fodla awaited the last of their enemies: Sinsar of the Battles and his son Borba, with all their men.

This was the fourth combat of the Ford of the Quicken Trees, and it was a hard fight that continued all day and did not stop at sunset. But Diarmuid and Fodla, in a momentary lull in the fighting, spoke to each other, and Diarmuid advised that they should hold off from attacking with equal ferocity to their enemy's and save their strength until help arrived or until Fionn could join with them.

In the early light of dawn, there came against Diarmuid and Fodla not only Sinsar and Borba, but also the King of the World with all his men. Things might have gone ill indeed with Diarmuid and Fodla, but that with the first ray of the sun, Fionn and Goll and the rest recovered back all their old strength. Chanting their battle cry, they joined in the fray. Things might still have gone ill for the weary defenders, if not that before the morning was passed, Oisin and the rest of the Fianna came upon the scene. With all his warriors at his side, Fionn rose up in his battle fury and inflicted such slaughter that few men lived to speak of their defeat.

Among the slain were both Sinsar and Borba, the sons of the King of the World. After that, it was a long time before any man of Ireland stood against the Fianna. But it was only after the battles, when the Fianna rode away from the Hostel of the Quicken Trees, which they left in flames, that Diarmuid remembered the words of the battle goddess he had carried on his shoulders long since and knew that this was the same ford where she had prophesized that a deed long remembered would be done.

TALIESIN AND THE SONG OF TRADITION

In the high places of the Land
Tradition's song continues,
Offering its unequalled orison
To all who listen,
beating down on the mirrored lake of dreams.

Here, the king's poet,
Taliesin of the Radiant Brow,
Utters a new blessing:
That all who seek,
That all who find,
May discover their wisdom,
Whether at the cauldron's rim
Or from the inward beating heart.

The poet's message
Flutters in the soul's cage
Like a bright bird;
The truth he utters
Echoes in the darkest corners,
Rings out from the highest dreaming spires
In the bright land.

With him, we come to the edge;
Remembering all he has given
We descend to a place
Of new turned earth.

16
SINGER

It is not hard to see why this story should be included here, for it tells of another great singer who, like the noble Taliesin, wrought magic with words and song. The tale of that singer, who is named Orfeo, has been told often before, yet here the teller speaks as one who was present. Perhaps this is one of those instances in which the great bard shows his ability to be present in other times, to move from place to place by subtle ways. Even to think of this feat causes me to grow fearful, for such skills are practiced only by those who are in league with the Dark One. Yet such is the power of the Lord Taliesin's spirit that I cannot believe him to be such a one. Therefore, though I am uncertain of the source of this tale, I place it here with others of unknown origin, in the hope that those who read it in future time will better understand its purpose.

ight gleamed fitfully in the globes that hung suspended between shadowy pillars in the great hall. Peacocks strutted fretfully on the chequered floor, fanning their great-eyed tails, heavy with pearls. A tree with strange-ly shaped fruit cast shifting lights on the face of the king, purple

shadows that moved and flickered over his blue-black hair. His eyes were half-closed, their gleam reddish beneath lowered lids. His hands moved restlessly on velvet covered knees.

The Singer knew all these things, yet saw none of them. Eyes closed, his hands stroked the strings of his harp as though it were a living thing—as perhaps it was, for surely there was knowledge in the gleaming eyes set into the face that decorated the great curved prow of the instrument.

On a low couch behind the king's chair, a woman moved softly in her sleep. Deep purple shadows lay upon her eyes, and her dreams, of a far-away place, reflected on her face like hurrying clouds. The music of the Singer reached her from a thousand miles off, and a thousand years of sleep stretched behind her in seeming. For she dreamed of things but lately come to her, as yet distantly, and in her sleeping vision walked under different skies and remembered another time, another place.

The Singer, suspended in his own dream spinning, felt himself both present in that timeless place and far away. Though his hands caressed the harp, he no longer knew how long he had played or why he continued to do so. He knew only that he must play until the king grew weary or until time itself came to an end. Yet the music freed him as, perhaps, it freed the king—and in that freedom he walked the same landscape as the woman, and they were together in another place, walking.

There, under skies innocent of fear, the man and the woman walked with arms entwined. She, looking up at the face above her, smiled. But a shadow fell between them, a dark and shapeless terror that stalked their world, and then suddenly, the man was alone on the green hillsides, head bent in sorrow, the weight of loneliness on his bowed shoulders.

Then, for a time, the harp was his only companion, and he wandered in search of what he had lost, and where he wandered played such tunes as none might hear and not be moved. Then on a day the wanderer came to a place where tall rocks stood dark and silent beside a deep river that flowed from the lighted lands into tunnels of unending dark, down into the lightless places where the terror that had stolen away his love lived in shadowy splendor amid towers of crystal and bone.

After many days, during which he sat solitary on the edge of the stream, the wanderer grasped the harp tightly in his arms and cast himself adrift upon the wild waters, which swept him downward until he came at last to the lightless lands. There he walked on the black sand by a lake of pearls, playing and playing until the sound of his music reached at last the ears of a king long grown weary of his silent court.

And thus the wanderer became the Singer, seated at the foot of the dark throne, while the peacocks turned and turned, and the light gleamed in the pearly globes that hung like lamps in the black arches of the chequered hall. Beyond them lay room upon room, hall after hall, filled with dreamers whose sleep was as endless and as timeless as the king who held them all in thrall. Though not himself asleep like the rest, as he played the Singer felt himself suspended, held fast in the king's mind, another reflection chained in a mirror.

Yet now at last, as the Singer played, the glimmer of a new thought furrowed the brows of the monarch, threads of change entered his eyes, and in the most distant part of the palace, the sleepers turned restlessly on their couches of dream— though near at hand they slept still deeper. In her dream, too, the woman felt a change beginning; the scenes that crept within her mind grew troubled. Like a breath of wind on the still water of a lake, small ripples spread outward, growing larger, and in the pattern of her deepest thoughts, an image appeared of one she loved, whose fingers stroked her face like the strings of a harp.

And still the Singer played, until at last, in the topmost roof of the lightless world, a tiny chink of light appeared, and spread, and was a star; within the star was the face of a woman, strange and unearthly, pale as a moon, looking down with far-seeing eyes that penetrated to the depths of that ancient realm.

In his chair of dreams the king stirred, moved where movement had ceased long ages since, turning up sightless eyes towards that far-off glimmer. On the tree of strange fruit that grew out of the chequered floor, two fruit, like globes of moonlight, glowed brightly, and the leaves, touched by the tones of the harper's song, stirred in the breathless wind. Like time itself, stilled to a snail's animation, the fruit detached themselves from the branches and began to fall to earth. In that moment the Singer ceased his song, the player played no longer, and the King of Dreams stirred at last and looked to where the fruit lay broken on the ground.

With hands that trembled, he reached down, dabbled his fingers in the spilled juice, and pressed them to his eyes. All time hung still in the lightless realm, as dreamers held for a thousand years felt a new pattern enter their ages-long sleep. At length the monarch sighed, and rising to his feet, cast his shadow-self into the fountain which bubbled where the tree had stood. Like curtains lifting, the shadows fled, and light, long banished, entered the windows of the halls of night. In countless rooms the sleepers stirred, raised their heads and looked around, seeking the dying echoes of the harper's song. While from the fountain came echoes of laughter, and stars pricked out in the heaven of the woken world.

TALIESIN'S QUEST

(1)

In a wood heavy with violets
I wandered in search of the star
I had marked in its passage
Down the sky. But the trees
Were dark, kept their secrets
In heavy silence, hung down
Their crabbed boughs,
Writhed their thick roots,
Moaned to themselves, tormented.

(2)

On a lake of moon-broken water
I sailed in search of the light
I had seen gleaming
Through torn cloud-wrack
Above the mountain's eye.
But the wind knifed through me
As though it would sever soul from body,
And the water was too dark
To hold my reflection.

(3)

In a deep-delved cave
I sought the twisted shadow
I had marked in torchlight
Where it played on crystal walls,
Reflecting the faces of those

Who had hunted there before.
But the torchlight flickered
And went out, and having not
The noctule sight of those
Who went before, I failed to see
The water where the dark wood lay.

17
THE FALLING

How often have I heard a brother reading aloud to us in the dining hall from the Great Book tell of the fall of the rebellious angels, led by one named Lucifer. When I first read the story that follows here, it shocked and disturbed me greatly, for does it not suggest that this fallen angel suffered greatly, even so much as we have been taught we might suffer if we were to choose, as some have done, to follow him? Also, unless I read it wrongly, it suggests that the fallen one is almost heroic in his struggle against the Beast, surely Satan himself? Then, too, I wonder at words that seem to echo the mystery of the Grail, written of elsewhere in this collection. ❧ All of this is strange to me, as are the lines that I found, written in an unfamiliar hand, on the back of the parchment on which the tale was scrawled: "This I saw and thus I write." I do not know what these words portend, or even if they have any part in the story, but I record them here in case those who come after me may understand them better than I. Nor do I know whether this tale was written by the Lord Taliesin or is another of those tales added by another hand. Whatever its source, the story is terrible in its power—of that much, at least, I am certain.

He hung on the edge of the sky like a tear in the eye of a queen.

Then he fell, and the darkness enclosed him, wrapping him round in its sticky webs. Only the bright glow of his sword, held out before him like a torch, illumined his path—the path that was no path, the direction that was without direction, the goal that was unknown to him because he has not been given any chance to consider it.

Words had been expunged from his mind, so that he no longer possessed the language to formulate speech. Only a last brief glimpse of the Sword of Flame seared into his brain, and the sense of the Shaper's thoughts rang in his mind. "You are no longer my Son. You have betrayed me. There is no place here for you. Begone!"

Then there was only the falling, the darkness, and a silence that was made worse because somewhere, like a distant echo, he heard singing—knew it was singing, even though he had no words for it, and longed to join his own voice to those of the Others. But he neither knew, nor could remember, who the Others were, who the Shaper was, and why he could still see, like a last echoing cry, a flash of red wings. His own were white, shading to gold. He knew this, even though he could see nothing in the darkness. Nor could he turn his head. His eyes seemed fixed, looking forward at the green glitter of his sword.

Gradually, so gradually that, at first, it was no more than a vague sensation in the deepest recesses of his mind, he became aware of a change in the texture of the darkness. In some way, though he groped for concepts to fashion the thought, somehow the darkness was growing thicker. His descent began, imperceptibly, to slow.

And then ahead, giving for the first time dimension to his fall, he saw something else, something that was not himself nor his sword—a dim, distant break in the darkness, as though someone had thrust a pin through the vast velvet drape and let in a ray light—always supposing that there was light somewhere beyond the endless seeming dark.

Slowly the dim glint took on shape and substance. A tiny whirling ball of light and shadow, intricately patterned with spirals of what, in some fashion, he

THE FALLING

knew to be earth and water. The ball lay before him, captured in an eddy of time and space into which he fell like a stone into a pool.

The noise of his landing must have woken the heavens themselves but raised no echoes. Its effect upon him was, however, vast. He found that he could hear. Sounds filled his head and, with them, came words that gave them substance. He stood upon something he knew to be "sand," saw "waves" strike a "shore," felt a thousand glimmering droplets touch his face as "rain," something within him said.

His other senses followed in quick succession. Smell came first, and with it a tang of salt air and a scent he associated at once with greenness and growth. In his ears rang the sound of the waves hammering at the sandy shoreline.

His fingers relaxed around the hilt of his sword, as the sensation of touch returned, and he realized that he had been gripping the weapon as though everything depended upon it. He looked at the bright blade and saw the green flame still lit within its faceted and polished surfaces. Its use fascinated him. It had seemed no more than a beacon, but now he knew it for a weapon that could be used for a purpose he did not yet understand.

Reflexively, he arched his wings and felt the play of the wind within them. He looked up at the sky and found its blueness pleasing. A bright bead of light shone down upon him. He stretched out his hands to touch it, only to find that it was too far. A sadness overtook him; a sense of loss.

He stood thus for a long time, while the bright bead of light fell down the sky (fell, like himself?) and turned slowly to crimson. At his feet the sea turned first purple and then the color of milk. He raised his eyes and saw another globe of light hanging where the other had been. This one was closer, imbued with a satiny white sheen. Again, he reached towards it and, again, found it beyond his touch.

Then, as he looked with longing and sorrow towards the light, something came between it and himself. A shadow, formless at first, but slowly taking shape. Winged, like himself, but different. A long neck and a hideous head. Somehow he knew that he was beautiful and that this winged form, whatever it was, was dark and misshapen, while he was light and made according to the Shaper's will.

With this thought came the sense of his own ability. The sword rose in his hand, and the green flame leaped within it as though at his unspoken command. The winged shadow spied it and turned upon him a concentrated beam of such malevolence that it was as though a breath of fire had struck at him. Almost, he staggered. But then an answering strength awoke within him, and he sent forth a ray of green radiance from his sword hand that broke upon the shadow's front and sent it roiling backwards upon itself.

But only for a moment. The Beast (for such he now knew the shadowed shape to be) uncoiled its vast length and struck downwards at him with a speed that seemed impossible for its size. A lash of pure fear struck him, and pain awoke within him. So new was the sensation that he scarcely felt it at first. But hate awoke next and knowledge of a deeper kind than before, and he knew that here was purpose, where before there had been only emptiness.

Without thought he drew back the hand in which his sword was grasped and flung it forward and upwards at the shadow above him. Trailing a tail of green fire, the sword flashed through the darkness and struck deep within the heart of the Beast. A terrible soundless cry echoed across the face of the sky, and the ground beneath his feet trembled and seemed itself to cry out. The Beast spun away into blackness, its terrible body ruptured and hurt beyond healing.

A moment of stillness brought back to his mind the silence of his long fall. Then the ground shook again and a fissure opened beneath his feet. As he fell— again, falling!—he caught a final glimpse of the sword. It had passed through the Beast, or perhaps had been disgorged by it. Now it arced across the sky like a comet, trailing green fire. Then it was gone from his sight, and the rushing darkness and warmth of the earth held him in a fast embrace.

Somewhere he became aware of a voice that spoke out of the darkness. "Come. Sleep. Be at one with me. Let us dream together."

At once he knew peace, such peace as he had never thought to know again. After millennia of wakefulness, he could sleep at last. And dream.

And in his dream he saw again the sword flash in the heavens, curving upward until it could go no further, then falling back towards the place where he had stood in contemplation of the new world of which he was now a part. As it fell, the texture of the air through which the sword passed thickened, driving the point back upon itself, the hilts curving outward to form an enclosing rim. Before it reached the earth, the sword had a new form entirely—a green cup-shaped vessel, from which something of the green light of its former shape still shone, though dimmer now. It came to rest at last on a table of stone, a vast flat-topped mountain that rose out of the warm lands like a fist. There it rested, and there, for a time, he lost sight of it.

Thus began his dream, which encompassed long ages. Many things there were to see in that time—the coming of men and their growing knowledge of good and evil, light and dark. Sometimes he was able to speak to one or another of them and heard his name—a name he had never answered to before—cursed for the knowledge he offered.

And at last, after ages of darkness, he saw the cup that had been formed from his sword taken up and wielded by hands other than his own. Then it was lost, and he saw men set forth in search of it, following a last subtle gleam of the old light—no longer green, but silvered now, like the color of old bone. He knew that one day it would be found again, and that while the search continued, it would not be forgotten. This thought gave him some comfort as he lay, between waking and sleeping, in the arms of the earth, listening always for the voices of the Others whose song he would one day rejoin.

TALIESIN THE SHAMAN

Half-in
half-out of the worlds
I'm caught
like a shadow
cut from its source
dreaming
dreaming
shifting shape

Into and
out of the worlds
I dance
like a candle flame
caught
by the wind

I'm half-dream,
half-real;
what am I?
that the wind knows
that the moon knows
that the earth knows
that they never tell!

18

MAZE

nce I made a journey to find the truth about a journey. I have never forgotten it. It was long before the days of King Arthur, or of the Grail, during the time when I still studied the shape of the mysteries at the little community founded by Myrddin's teacher Blaise at Ystrad Fawr. It was before I understood the nature of the Wood, or how my own path was destined to lead there. When I close my eyes I can see it now, the road opening before me, and I see him beckoning me on, the Man in the Maze, with star and staff. ❧ Though I'm not certain what to do, I go anyway, where he leads, and find myself among the branching ways, the night tracks and the day tracks, all a-snuffle with badger and hedge pig, while overhead the birds work to and fro, bright shuttles on a loom of branches. He's always before me, the man, with his bright staff leading me on and the star bright as can be, at times before, at times behind, at times overhead. And I follow, like a wise man on route to Bethlehem, though not knowing where. ❧ I find myself going along a spiral way, uphill towards a place of stones gathered into a huddle, from which they look out all round at the land. I stand there, too, and look about me. I see the rolling hills, the grass growing on them next to the wheat, all waving in the wind like a green and golden sea.

"What am I come for?" I ask the man, but he only smiles without saying and points to where the star has gone before, settled now over the shadow of a little vale between the hills.

"Am I to go there?" I ask the man, and he smiles and points.

It takes me a while to get to the vale, but in the end I find myself standing between the hills. A spring breaks out of the hillside and runs away towards a place where the stones form a maze. I take some water in my hands and drink. I hear the sound of singing that comes from somewhere near, and I look up to see that the star sits now directly overhead. I go forward to see what I can see.

I make for a little sheltered spot between some bushes and a strand of trees. From there, light shows in the dark, which has come on fast since I started out. I see a low building made of old stone with a door and a window set in it. Approaching, I hear a voice say, "Come in."

This is what I see: Three people gathered around a table. One is the Man in the Maze, smiling still. (Though how he got there before me, I cannot say). Another is a queenly woman, with a silence in her. The third is a boy, who looks not at me but at the table, on which there is something I can't quite see, though I look and look.

I want to leave, feeling suddenly shy, as though this moment was something secret to those three. But the woman looks my way, smiles, and beckons me in, so I go closer and try again to see what is on the table.

It changes so fast I can't quite catch it. But I see something of it: The shape of a salmon, of a kingfisher, of a little dog. Then a hen with her chicks, and a cock in all his finery. Last of all is a babe, and he has such a light about him that I am frightened, then consoled, finally joyful. His name comes to me unbidden: Mabon, the Son of the Mother. For he looks at me straight, and I hear, not with words, but inside me, thoughts that form a song:

I am in the world.
I am outside the world.
I am true to all who seek me.
I am true to all who do not.
I am a shadow, a dewdrop,
A beam of sun, a leaf.
I am in all things,
Upon the wind's back I fly,
And in the streams and rivers swim.
I move in the earth
And I walk upon it.
One is one, alone.
Ever to be. Ever me.

Looking up, I see only the woman and the Man in the Maze, who smiles at me still and points toward the door. Then I am back on the road, remembering everything clearly. I have broken the pattern. The maze is inside me now. I have broken its pattern by making it part of me. The song of the child is part of me, too, and I remember the look of the man and of the woman who called me.

It's good to be on the road again, to see it stretching before me garbed in white dust, and the fields on either side full of golden wheat, and the trees beckoning with the promise of shade ahead. I still have far to go.

There is so much that is mysterious here that I cannot even begin to fathom it. All I can think is that the babe at the heart of this mystery is, indeed, the blessed Mabon, whom all now know as the Christ. It gladdens my heart to think that Taliesin knew this mystery and fled not from it.

THE DREAM OF MACSEN WLELDIG

Macsen, from his pillow of shields,
In dream went far upon the road,
Crossed mountains to reach the sea,
And on the sea took ship.
On the shore of a green island

He landed, by the walls of a castle,
In whose hall he found
An old man carving chessmen,
And two youths, who fought
A silent duel on the board,
While in a chair of purest silver
With lion arms and eagle's feet,
A girl whose gold outshone the sun
Sat waiting for his eager step.

He awoke to rattle of spears
And whimper of hound, to find
The dream unkindly false.
But after, true to memory,
He rose, and sailed,
Proved true the dream,
Discovering his empress
On a mountain stair.

19
THE THIRD AWAKENING

*O*nce again I must confess that this story makes me fearful, as do many that are gathered here. What is described is not hard to understand, although it is written obliquely, but surely by one who has known this mystery for himself. For does this tale not say plainly that there are those who live upon this earth who have lived before, and will live again, and so on until the wheel ceases to turn? Yet this teaching I know to be heresy, and I tremble at the thought of a soul so bound. ❧ As with many of the parchments I discovered long since, this tale is not written in the hand of the little monk, nor of the bard himself, so that I have no knowledge of who wrote it or when. That it belongs at the end of this collection seems clear enough. Almost it seems to usher in a whole new chapter in the chronicle of ancient times that was the final testimony of the Lord Taliesin.

here was darkness again. And then a sound like an ebbing roar, withdrawing into the innermost recesses of his mind, taking with it light, sound, voices. The screams of the dying? If this is death, then it is a

peaceful country. But it was not, not this time, not yet, and that certainty was like a raft to hold onto as he rode the sea of darkness towards some other place.

It had been different the first time. Then he had not gone willingly, had fought the hands that pushed him into the unknown, the fearful, where he knew only that he was no longer completely himself, that another consciousness had entered the place where the small gleed of light that was solely his still dwelled.

Then there had been light, and smoke that made his eyes weep, and voices chanting, and he had been raised up until he stood in a high place, looking down at the land and hearing in his head the other consciousness telling him that this was his task, the care and guarding of this small piece of the whole, a piece important despite its smallness, a place made sacred by the presence of a sleeper within the earth.

He had been shown the same place from a still greater height, and now he saw it as an island of light amid a great sea of darkness (like that on which he now rode, borne up by the knowledge that soon he would wake). And in that sea were creatures of the dark, who belonged there because they loved to be where there was no light, who hated the land and sought to overwhelm it forever so that all might be dark together.

Then he had known fear such as he had never felt when facing a physical enemy, and had screamed aloud, and woken. But all that had happened the first time. The second awakening had been less terrible, though the events he recalled from it were nonetheless dark.

Having been there once, he was prepared, knowing the signs, feeling the approach of that other consciousness and the darkening of all perspectives, until all that remained was a pinprick of awareness like a bubble floating on an ocean of night. But then, after a time, had come fear—for the voice had not spoken, and the night had remained dark, and all sound was stolen, leaving him more alone than ever before.

Madness might have come, but for the faint radiance that shone deep within him that marked the edges of his consciousness. And then he dreamed that the island had been overcome and that the creatures of the dark ocean were crawling forth to devour all that was left of the light. But that had not happened. There was a sense, even in the silence of his prison, of warmth and gentle harboring that kept him buoyed up through his long sleep.

For that was how it seemed then, a sleep and a rest that gathered the essence that was himself closer around him. After a time, the memories of those who were close to him returned, and the love of woman and friend, so that he was no longer alone. Finally, there was speech also, and the familiar voice that spoke to him of giving up things that others might possess freedom.

Supported thus, he had found the courage to frame words of his own—a question, a name sought for in the dark.

"I am the helper," came the whispered reply. "I am he who turns the wheel upon which the Pendragon sits."

With that word, that naming, had come many kinds of understanding. Recognition woke within him of other times and other names, while always the dark dragon coiled in and around the cup from which he drank, imbibing knowledge and forgetfulness at the hands of the helper.

That knowledge stood him in good stead through the trials and tests that followed his second wakening. It shaped the outline of the destiny he strove to follow and softened the blows that took away so much of the dream.

But in the end had come again the blast of light, the down draught of air that meant release . . . the rapid plash of water and the arched back of the salmon . . . the voices of his men calling him forth . . . or was that another dream? In the darkness, he could no longer be sure. For this was the third sleeping, the third period of Oeth and Anoeth, of hidden and unknown, of lost and found.

Many things were shown him in that time, and above all else he saw with the clarity of desire a face, dim at first as though the clay was still unformed, but growing sharper, clearer, until his successor stood forth, clearly revealed. When it did, he knew that his imprisonment in the tower had been for a purpose, that the dark ocean with its creatures would not yet overwhelm the island of light, and that his work had not been in vain.

When, after a time, the light returned, he was almost afraid to look. But then he saw that his own hands, which before had been gnarled and knotted with age, were now smooth and strong. He felt exultation, which flowed into and through him until he stood, at last, facing a new day.

Then one came whom he knew; though until that moment, he had never seen the face. The helper stood before him laughing and said, "Come forth. A new Pendragon has been chosen, and the wheel has turned for the last time."

And Arthur went forth into Avalon.

TALIESIN'S MADNESS

The poet crept
into the mind of the king
urging him to find
the truth behind the fires
that danced in his head.

Taliesin, winged, fled
across the dreaming land
seeking answers
to the broken things.

He fell, and with him
the dream of Logres
shattered into fragments
too small to find again.

NOTES AND SOURCES

hese stories draw upon the mythical history of Dark Age and Medieval Britain. For readers who seek a deeper understanding of these matters or who wish to explore the source material, I include these notes intended to point to the sources of these tales, where such are known, and to illuminate some of their more obscure details.

1: JOSCELYN'S TALE

This story, which frames the rest, places the fictional gathering of the stories in the thirteenth century, when the monk Joscelyn is said to have lived. Ynys Witrin, Joscelyn's monastery, is, of course, Glastonbury, where there was, indeed, a magnificent abbey with a very fine library, broken up during the English Civil War when the abbey itself was destroyed.

Rumors about "a certain book, written in the British Tongue" were in circulation earlier than this. The cleric Geoffrey of Monmouth claimed that his own *History of the Kings of Britain*, which provided source material for many later writers, including Shakespeare, was a translation of this ancient book. No trace of this chronicle has ever come to light, however, and many scholars presume that it was, as was the case for so many suggested literary antecedents at this time, invented by a medieval author to provide authority for his work. However, there is no reason at all why such a book should not have existed, and I have extended this speculation to back up the story.

The discovery of the grave of Arthur did take place, as described, in 1190. King Edward I visited Glastonbury in 1278 and had the bones reinterred in a marble tomb, as Joscelyn tells. This tomb was later destroyed, but a plaque marking its believed site can still be seen among the ruins of Glastonbury Abbey.

2: THE KINGLY SHADOW

In this story a meeting takes place between two men, one of whom already rules the kingdom of Britain and the other who will do so in a time to come.

Kings and kingship were always sacred matters to the people of Britain. Descriptions still exist of ceremonies in which the king symbolically married the land, either in the shape of an otherworldly woman who represented the Goddess of the island, or, as in Ireland, in which the king mated with a white mare in whose blood he ritually bathed and whose flesh he afterwards consumed. A description of this ceremony can be read in Giraldus Cambrensis' book, *Journey Through Ireland* (1191).

Ambrosius Aurelianus, who held together the war-torn kingdom of Britain in the inter-regnum between the demise of Vortigern (the Gwytheryn of this story) and the coming of Arthur, was perhaps of mixed Roman and British blood, though there are hints that Ambrosius' family may have been of imperial stock. If he was, indeed, of mixed native and Roman blood, this ancestry may have been of great advantage in enabling him to weld both peoples into a force strong enough to repel the invading Saxons, Picts, and Scots until the time when Arthur arrived on the scene.

Of Ambrosius' life and death, little is known. The period in which he lived was one of great turmoil, and there is little in the way of verbatim reports; most chronicles covering the period 460–85 (roughly the time of Ambrosius' campaign) date from several centu-ries after this time. The sixth-century monk Nennius, in his *History of Britain*, calls Ambrosius *Emrys Wledig* or "Overlord" and relates the story of Vortigern's tower with Ambrosius as the opponent of that treacherous king, thereby aligning Ambrosius, the warlord, with Merlin (*Myrddin Emrys*), the mysterious prophet. Geoffrey of Monmouth, in his *History of the Kings of Britain* (c. 1105), drew fruitfully upon this confusion as well as upon the oral traditions relating to Merlin.

Certainly there is a strong line of tradition connecting Ambrosius and Arthur, which the story related here sustains. Whether any such meeting as the one described in it ever took place is, of course, a matter for speculation.

3: THE BRIDE OF THE SPEAR

This story is based upon the oldest traditions reflected in this collection. The first speaker is clearly intended to be Taliesin. Though the story has no single source, it contains many references to the ancient tradition of the Wasteland, which features widely in texts dealing with the quest for the Grail. In the earliest sources, the Wasteland comes about because of some unspecified failing on the part of the king. Later texts say that the king's failing is a wound, generally in the thighs, that makes him unable to father children or to fulfill his kingly duties. The assumption in some of the Arthur legends is that he himself was such a wounded king and that Britain was for a time a Wasteland, which was healed only by the discovery of the Grail. The most famous literary exponent of the Wasteland theme was T. S. Eliot, whose seminal poem "The Wasteland" trans-formed twentieth-century poetry. Eliot drew on the writings of anthropologist Jessie L.

Weston, whose great book *From Ritual to Romance* (1920) explored the theme of the Wasteland in depth.

Beyond these sources, the story reflects the very ancient themes of sacrifice and of the deep connection that once existed between humanity and the earth. This same theme is expressed in a number of the earlier Arthurian tales collected here, such as "Owein of the Ravens," "The Island of Sorrow and Joy," and "The Abduction and Rescue of Gwenhywfar the Queen."

4: IN THE PRISON OF ARIANRHOD

This strange tale, or grouping of tales, predates the time of Arthur by many hundreds of years. Yet in many ways, it springs from the same ancient fertility rites as those mentioned in "The Bride of the Spear." The names Elcmar, Boand, and Oengus are well known from Irish myth, in which Elcmar is the human husband of the goddess Boand, who gives birth to the god of love, Oengus mac Og.

These names are meant to suggest a link between the Arthurian and Irish mythic cycles, a connection suggested elsewhere in the parallels between the Celtic Hallows and the symbols found in the later Grail myths. The Hallows are four sacred objects described in the eleventh-century Irish *Book of Invasions* that are deeply connected to the health of the land. They are: the sword of Nuadu, the spear of Lugh, the cauldron of the Dagda, and the stone of Fal. Perceptive readers will find variations of these four symbols throughout the stories in this collection and see in them parallels to such schemes as the four suits of the Tarot. In later tellings of the Arthurian tales, the symbols were often Christianized, such that the sword belongs to John the Baptist and the spear to Longinus, the cauldron becomes the Grail, and the stone becomes a chessboard. American scholar A. C. L. Brown comments at some length on these parallels in his book *The Origin of the Grail Legend* (Cambridge, Mass.: Harvard University Press, 1943).

The suggestion that Taliesin may have known something of the Irish stories is born out by references to Irish myth within his surviving poetry. There is also a suggestion, hinted at here, that the story of Elcmar and Boand may parallel Arthur's own initiation by his half-sister Morgause into the mysteries of kingly marriage to the land. The story also bears out the idea that Taliesin was, as I believe, an initiate of still older mysteries than those of his own time. Finally, in combining these fragments into a single tale, I am trying to suggest ancient beliefs about the connection between man's fertility and that of the earth.

5: THE ISLAND OF SORROW AND JOY

It is often wrongly assumed that only men went on quests or had adventures in the Arthurian world. In fact, women played an extremely important role in the whole Arthurian mythos, and one in particular, Dindraine, the sister of Perceval, sacrificed herself for another lady and thus enabled the three Grail knights to achieve their quest on behalf of the whole realm of Logres. As told in Sir Thomas Malory's *Le Morte D'Arthur* (1485), Dindraine's body was carried by the three successful Grail knights to the holy city of Sarras, where she was buried along with Galahad, after he achieved the mysteries—the first man and woman of earthly lineage to be interred there, though Malory never names the lady, calling her only "Perceval's sister."

There is a sense in which Dindraine represents Guinevere (Gwenhwyfar) Arthur's queen, in the same way that the wounded king in the Grail legends stands as a surrogate for Arthur himself. The relationship between king and land is one of the deepest themes of this book, as reflected in this story, as well as in "Drustan's Ghost" and "The Bride of the Spear." In the story of Drustan, we see how the planned marriage between king and land is thwarted by the love that grows between Drustan and Issylt. In "The Bride of the Spear," the love between the Spear Maiden and the harper Lugaid goes against the rules of the ritualized society. The pair's sacrilege (like the illicit love between Guinevere and Lancelot) is given as one of the causes of the Wasteland and explains the wounding of the Grail king.

In "The Island of Sorrow and Joy," set on the sacred island of Iona off the western coast of Scotland, we see a kind of solution to the dilemma posed by these stories, in that the queen (Dindraine/Guinevere) offers a blood sacrifice for the sake of both king and land.

6: LUGH OF THE STRONG ARM AND THE THREE QUEENS

In the medieval romances, the figure of Sir Lancelot of the Lake stands at the forefront of Arthur's knights. He displaced earlier heroes, such as Gawain and Cei, and became the premier knight of the Round Table, unbeaten in single combat or tournament until the coming of his strange and saintly son Galahad, the Grail winner.

Many scholars have followed the belief that Lancelot sprang from the fertile brain of French poet Chretien de Troyes, who wrote at the end of the twelfth century. However, an alternative theory suggests that behind the figure of the medieval knight stands a succession of older, Celtic heroes, of the kind more appropriate to the historical period in which Arthur lived.

Among the most prominent of these are Lugh Loinnbheimionach and Llwch Llemineawg, originally the same character but subsequently split into Irish and Welsh versions. Both were noted for their strength, fiery disposition, and the possession of magical weapons—a spear that roared for blood in the case of the Irish Lugh, and a flaming sword in that of the Welsh Llwch.

The story told here is based on one of the most famous episodes from the life of Lancelot—his encounter with three magical women of Arthurian Britain. However, in this version, it is Lancelot's earlier self, Lugh, who is the protagonist.

The three queens themselves—in the medieval version Morgan le Fay, Morgana, and the unnamed Queen of Norgalles—can be seen as representing ancient Celtic matriarchal figures, who are, at a deeper level, aspects of the Triple Goddess, worshiped throughout the Western world during the Bronze Age and after.

The description of the otherworldly realm in which Lugh/Lancelot is imprisoned is consistent with details found in many Celtic stories, as is the belief that, while the denizens of Faery may capture the body of human beings, they have no power over their souls, and thus cannot compel them to act against their will.

Time is either without meaning or of a different order in Faery. When the Irish hero Bran son of Febal visited the Land of Women (a place not unlike the realm in which Lugh is here confined), he remained there for what seemed to him only a few months, but when he returned to the real world, he found all whom he had known to be long dead. He himself had become legendary.

The final paragraph of the story refers to another episode from the life of Lancelot—how a maiden from the land of Astolat fell in love with him and how, when her passion was unrequited, she died and her body was ferried down river to the walls of Camelot, together with a letter that told her story. In Malory's *Le Morte D'Arthur*, this sad tale becomes part of the romance of chivalry and courtly love. In the nineteenth century, Alfred Lord Tennyson retold it in his narrative poem *The Lady of Shalott*. The version offered here suggests another origin for the story.

7: OWEIN OF THE RAVENS

The story of Owein of the Ravens, or as it is more properly called, "Rhonabwy's Dream," comes from the premier source for ancient Welsh lore and legend known as *The Mabinogion*. The source story contains, perhaps, the most significant descriptions of Arthur's warriors—

not, as one might expect, couched in the language or fashion of the twelfth century, when it was written down, but bearing all the marks of the sixth-century warriors, upon whom Arthur's knights are based. The intricate and detailed descriptions of clothing and weapons in the *Mabinogion* story are unparalleled and are the reason why this story is said to be impossible to tell from memory, as the ancient bardic storytellers once did with their lore and history.

Owein himself appears in the medieval romances as Sir Uwain, the son of Arthur's greatest adversary, King Urien of Gore. In fact, both Urien and Owein are historically attested figures, both of whom had bardic laments written about them that are still extant. Urien was king of the Strathclyde area of northern Britain, either in the same period or shortly after that of Arthur. An early Welsh lament commemorating Owein's death describes him as "reaper of foes" and "a despoiler."

Much speculation has gone into the nature of the strange game played by Arthur and Owein in this story. It is clearly a board game related to chess, though the scholarly consensus is that it is not chess. Another line of speculation points to the Irish game of *fidchel*. Little more is known about this game than about *gwyddbwyll*, but the identification does offer one clue into the nature of the conflict between Arthur and Owein. In fidchel, as in chess, the king is the most important piece and is defended by a series of knights; however, significantly, the king's defenders are fewer in number than his adversary's, whose task it is to capture him. If we assume that gwyddbwyll was a similar game, that Arthur was the king (in both senses of the word), and Owein's Ravens his opponents, we begin to see the story in a new light.

In the version of the story told here, as in the *Mabinogion* version, the battle between Arthur and his nephew is a symbolic or magical struggle carried on within the framework of a dream. Here the suggestion is that the Ravens were an actual group of fighting men, although in the original story, the literal meaning of the Ravens is ambiguous enough to give one pause. Ravens were the symbol of the Celtic battle goddess, the Morrigan, and references to the bloody work of these battleground scavengers suggest that the horrors of war may be the underlying theme of the tale. Perhaps also buried within the old text is a reference to the difficulties experienced by Arthur in trying to weld the proud, wild, passionate-natured Celtic tribesmen into a fighting unit alongside the Romano-British descendants of the Legions who had always been the tribesmen's enemy.

8: DRUSTAN'S GHOST

The central idea underlying this story is the marriage of the land and the king. This mystical relationship worked on two levels: the king mediated his rulership via his relationship with the Goddess of the land, Lady Sovereignty, but he also derived his kingship from the sovereignty bestowing maiden whom he married. In earlier times, in fact, it was the queen who descended from a holy bloodline and who chose a suitable husband to be her consort.

The story of Tristan, Iseult, and King Mark has always seemed to mask a deeper reality than the tragic human love triangle. The version of the story given here reverts to earlier antecedents of these characters, Drustan and Marcus, who derive from Pictish Scotland. Instead of sending Drustan to Ireland, Marcus sends him to the Otherworld to fetch his bride. The implication is that only through a union with the Goddess can Marcus restore the Wasteland. Because of the love that grows between Drustan and Issylt, the dynastic mingling of the ancient blood of the Sidhe (the Faery Folk) with the royal house of Cornwall is unsuccessful in this tale. The task then falls to Arthur and Guinevere—another faery bride, for only as such can her role in the Arthurian canon be truly understood. As in this story, however, fate intervenes in the form of her meeting with a younger, more able man—Lancelot—who interposes himself between the king and the land, as did Drustan.

Thus an ancient pattern is endlessly rewoven, and the Wasteland persists until that most elusive of otherworldly redemptions—the Grail—is finally found and another sacrifice of royal blood—the death of Galahad—is demanded.

9: THE ABDUCTION AND RESCUE OF GWENHWYFAR THE QUEEN

One of the most famous stories in the Arthurian cycle tells of the kidnapping and rescue of Arthur's queen. Chretien de Troyes used this story as the basis for his first Arthurian poem, "The Knight of the Cart," in which it is Lancelot who has the task of rescuing his lady from the evil Meleagraunce. The same story is told, in short form, by Malory. But an earlier version than either of these, found in *The Life of Saint Gildas*, written by Caradoc of Lancarven in 1150, inspires the version given here.

In Caradoc's tale, as in the version told here, Arthur is the hero, ranged against a wily, slightly sinister adversary. As Caradoc tells it, it is Saint Gildas who intervenes to bring about the release of the queen, but it seems more fitting to me that Arthur recover his wife unaided. Though in the end, of course, it is Gwenhwyfar who resolves the impasse using a ploy borrowed from the Welsh story of Trystan and Essyllt.

Placing Arthur at center stage reminds us how much things changed between the original events of the sixth century and the fanciful stories of the Middle Ages. In the medieval tales, Arthur is often little more than a figurehead, the central point about which the legends and fables of more interesting characters constellate. So, too, pushing the whole story further back in time allows some interesting antecedents of the other characters in the tale to reappear. Sir Kay, for example, the braggart and buffoon of the medieval stories, becomes again Cei, a redoubtable hero who stands close to Arthur himself; and Meleagraunce, the arch-villain, becomes Melwas of the Summer Country, an ancient name for the Lord of the Otherworld among the Celtic people.

However, the actual story of the abduction and rescue of the queen dates back many millennia before the time of Arthur. It is a form of a well-known folklore motif known as "The Abduction of the Flower Bride." Guinevere, like Blodeuwedd in the *Mabinogion* tale "Math, Son of Mathonwy," has many similarities to the otherworldly bride created by magical means in that tale. Behind all of these, is an older seasonal myth in which the kings of summer and winter fight annually over possession of the spring maiden or bride of flowers. Also behind this story is the classical Greek myth of the abduction of Eurydice by Hades, god of the underworld. A version of that myth is retold by Taliesin in the story called "Singer."

Guinevere's amorous adventures, such as those in this story, may account for the unfavorable light in which she appears in many medieval Arthurian tales. Given the times, medieval tellers should have seen her as a noble figure of courtly love. Instead, the descriptions of her are rather unsympathetic, probably because many were written by clerics, who could hardly come out in favor of adultery. Thomas Malory's portrait of Guinevere in *Le Morte D'Arthur* is the most interesting psychologically, but the final impression one gets of her character is, perhaps, the famous answer given by a schoolgirl to a question about Arthur's queen: that she was "a lady much given to being run off with."

10: GRISANDOLE

The source of this story is an obscure text known as "The English Merlin," which dates from the fourteenth century and is probably a translation of an older French romance. The Early English Text Society published this work in 1889 in several volumes, edited by Henry Wheatley. The story told here offers Merlin's own account of the events.

11: THOMAS AND THE BOOK

This story derives from a curious introductory tale appended to the vast twelfth-century collection of Arthurian literature known as *The Vulgate Cycle*. This text, written in medieval French, spans the whole cycle of Arthur's reign and devotes hundreds of pages to a deeply theological interpretation of the Grail story. In the fifteenth century, Thomas Malory used it as source for *Le Morte D'Arthur*. My version casts the story as a kind of interior monologue, with the theme of showing that the things we look for hardest are often right under our noses. The text mentioned in the story, the *Perlesvaus*, does exist and was probably written in Glastonbury c. 1350. It tells the story of the Grail quest in a most mystical fashion, much in keeping with the tone of the text described here.

12: THE VISION OF THE MOTHER OF GOD

This story draws upon two previously unconnected episodes, one from the *Perlesvaus*, mentioned above; the other from the sixth-century chronicle of Nennius, mentioned above in connection with the story "The Kingly Shadow." In the former, Arthur has a vision of the Virgin; in the latter, he is said to have carried a shield with her icon on it during the great battle at Badon. It seems not unreasonable to connect the two incidents as is done in my retelling. As is the case with all the stories retold here, the themes are traditional to the cycle of tales known as "the Matter of Britain." A tale like this one might have been told by one of the many wandering storytellers who kept the myths of Arthur and the Grail alive through the Middle Ages. Its inclusion in Taliesin's retelling of the stories in the "ancient book" I have imagined that he penned suggests that later keepers of the manuscript added their own favorite tales.

13: GALAHAD AND THE HOLY THINGS

Perhaps the most perfect retelling of the Grail story is found in Thomas Malory's *Le Morte D'Arthur*. Malory reduces the prolix and wandering account in *The Vulgate Cycle* into a tight and powerful tale of mystical adventure, in which the strength of the human spirit is tested to the extreme. The story told here for the most part follows Malory, but adds details not found in his version. The language and style of this piece date it far later than the time of Taliesin, yet it has something of the same spirit. Readers of the companion collection to these stories, *The Song of Taliesin* (Quest Books, 2001) may see in the image of the dark castle to which Galahad ascends an echo of the tower of Arawn as described in the story "The Voyage to Annwn."

14: COLLEN AND THE LORD OF THE MOUND

Gwynn ap Nudd (pronounced "nith") is traditionally associated with the area of the Vale of Neath in Wales, which derives its name from Gwynn's father Nudd (in Welsh, *ap* means "son of"). The elder Nudd was a foster-son of the goddess Don or Danu, which implies that he was of human origin, though no story tells of his birth and fostering in the Otherworld. Another theory identifies Gwynn with the Irish hero, Fionn mac Cumhail, since both were warriors and huntsmen whose prowess was legendary. Fionn, however, is of purely mortal stock, while there is a wildness in Gwynn that marks him out as an Otherworld being. The poem quoted in the story is from "The Black Book of Carmarthen," one of the *Four Ancient Books of Wales*, edited by W. F. Skene (New York: AMS Press, 1984-5). The translation is my own.

15: THE HOSTEL OF THE QUICKEN TREES

This tale is drawn, more or less directly, from the epic cycle of tales dating from the early Middle Ages to the mid-nineteenth century built around the figure of Fionn mac Cumhail (pronounced "Finn MacCool"), a legendary hero familiar from both folktale and literature. Like Taliesin, he was a poet as well as a warrior, and a verse ascribed to him, "Fionn's Poem of Mayday," still survives.

The suggestion that Fionn is, in some way, linked to Taliesin comes from a complex etymology that associates the root of Fionn's name with the root of Taliesin's boyhood name *Gwion*. Both the Irish *fi* and Welsh *gwi* mean "white" or "fair." Thus both figures can be seen as exponents of the "white wisdom," a kind of magic associated with other figures with similar names in Celtic tradition.

In addition to this connection, both Fionn and Taliesin acquired wisdom from imbibing hot liquid. As is alluded to in the story, as the boy Gwion, Taliesin was given the task of stirring the bubbling cauldron of the goddess Ceridwen. When a drop of the hot potion she was brewing splashed on his thumb, Gwion put it into his mouth to cool the burn and immediately entered upon an initiatory journey. Fionn became wise in a similar way, when the liquid in which the salmon of wisdom was being cooked splashed on his thumb. Ever after, he could access this wisdom by sucking his thumb! Readers interested in pursuing the parallels further should consult my book *Taliesin: The Last Celtic Shaman* (Inner Traditions, 2002).

16: SINGER

This story grew out of my fascination with later medieval versions of the classical tale of Orpheus. A fourteenth-century narrative poem, *Sir Orfeo*, as well as several folksongs, draw upon the original Greek myth of the poet's visit to the Underworld to bring back his wife Eurydice who has been stolen by Hades, the ruler of that realm. *Sir Orfeo* follows the basic pattern of the classical story, but places it in a recognizable medieval European landscape. It seems fitting that this tale of the magic of a great singer and poet should be part of the tales concerning Taliesin.

17: THE FALLING

This story was inspired by two very different sources. The first is the suggestion, embedded in Wolfram von Eschenbach's twelfth-century romance *Parzival*, that the Grail was a stone from the crown of the angel of light, Lucifer, which fell to earth during a struggle between the angels of light and the forces of darkness that shook the very foundations of heaven. The other is a fragmentary Gnostic story, which describes the fall of Lucifer into matter and his battle with the apocalyptic Beast. At the conclusion of the struggle, Lucifer takes the place of the Beast in the heart of the world.

18: MAZE

This story was inspired by a painting by the contemporary Celtic artist Courtney Davis that shows a man standing at the center of a maze. The painting haunted me for years until I wrote this tale. I make it part of Taliesin's story because the Wood through which so many of the characters in his tales wander in search of love or adventure is itself a maze.

Mazes appear in many cultures. At one level, they always represent our spiritual journey, as we turn and return along the avenues of life in search of meaning and understanding. In this story, the journey through the maze represents at a deeper level the quest for the Grail, which undergoes a series of magical transformations in some versions of the story. Taliesin himself experienced a series of similar transformations during his own initiatory experience, as told in the story "The Cauldron-Born" in *The Song of Taliesin*.

One of the forms taken by the Grail is as an infant, who is linked here with the Celtic divine child Mabon. In medieval theology, Mabon and Christ became inextricably associated, hence Brother Joscelyn's ease in making the identification. Medieval writings often spoke of "Mary's Mabon," and the threesome seen in Taliesin's vision is unmistakably like the holy family at the heart of the Christmas story. Readers interested in reading more about Mabon may wish to consult Caitlin Matthews' *Mabon: The Divine Child of Light* (Inner Traditions, 2002).

19: THE THIRD AWAKENING

This story is based on an obscure reference in the Welsh *Triads*. The *Triads* are a collection of gnomic statements which served as a way of listing groups of stories under generic headings. Many of them date from Arthur's time, though they were not collected until the Middle Ages. In this reference, Arthur is spoken of as a prisoner. The text runs: "One [prisoner] who was more exalted than [any], was three nights in prison in caer Oeth and Anoeth . . . and three nights in an enchanted prison under the stone of Echymeint. This exalted prisoner was Arthur." (*Trioedd Ynys Prydein*. trans. R. Bromwich. Cardiff: University of Wales Press, 1978).

Oeth and Anoth are roughly the equivalent of *alpha* and *omega*, meaning the beginning and the end. My story suggests that Arthur's imprisonment is of no ordinary kind, but is, perhaps, a kind of *metempsychosis*, the transmigration of a soul from one body to another, a belief held by the druids. The implication of the story is that there may have been more than one hero named Arthur, all of whom carry the same soul. Arthur's second "awakening" encompasses the events associated with the legendary king by that name. The ending hints that Arthur's third and final awakening as the once and future king may take place at any time—even in our day.

QUEST BOOKS
are published by
The Theosophical Society in America,
Wheaton, Illinois 60189-0270,
a branch of a world fellowship,
a membership organization
dedicated to the promotion of the unity of
humanity and the encouragement of the study of
religion, philosophy, and science, to the end that
we may better understand ourselves and our place in
the universe. The Society stands for complete
freedom of individual search and belief.
For further information about its activities,
write, call 1-800-669-1571, e-mail olcott@theosmail.net,
or consult its Web page: http://www.theosophical.org

The Theosophical Publishing House
is aided by the generous support of
THE KERN FOUNDATION,
a trust established by Herbert A. Kern
and dedicated to Theosophical education.